The Beery-Buktenica

Developmental Test of Visual-Motor Integration

VMI

With Supplemental Developmental Tests of
Visual Perception and Motor Coordination

Administration, Scoring
and Teaching Manual

4th Edition

Keith E. Beery, Ph.D.

W9-CZO-084

MODERN CURRICULUM PRESS

For the Children

ISBN 0-8136-8716-0

Modern Curriculum Press
An Imprint of Modern Curriculum
A Division of Simon & Schuster
299 Jefferson Road, P.O. Box 480
Parsippany, New Jersey 07054-0480

1 2 3 4 5 6 7 8 9 10 11 12 PT 02 01 00 99 98 97

Contents

Tables and Figures

Tables

Figures

Summary

The *Developmental Test of Visual-Motor Integration,* or *VMI,* is a developmental sequence of geometric forms to be copied with paper and pencil. The purposes of the *VMI* are to help identify, through early screening, children who may need special assistance, to obtain needed services, to test the effectiveness of educational and other interventions, and to advance research. The full, 27-item *VMI* can be either group or individually administered in about 10 to 15 minutes and is used with preschool children through adults. An 18-item version is available for ages 3 to 7.

First published as the *VMI* in 1967, it is used for and enjoyed by children throughout the United States and in other countries. Research indicates that the *VMI* is virtually culture-free. Because children with different backgrounds often have widely varying degrees of experience with alphabets and numbers, geometric forms are used in the *VMI* rather than letter or numeric forms.

The *VMI* test itself has remained basically unchanged and retains all of the forms, characteristics, and strengths of the original edition. What is new in 1996 is the provision of two supplemental standardized tests, *VMI Visual Perception* and *VMI Motor Coordination.* The *VMI* is designed to assess the extent to which individuals can integrate their visual and motor abilities. The two new tests are provided in response to *VMI* users who wish to statistically compare an individual's *VMI* results with relatively pure visual and motor performances. The new tests use the same stimulus forms as the *VMI,* unlike other visual-motor test batteries that mistakenly attempt to compare less related stimuli and tasks.

In order to directly compare *VMI* and supplemental test results, norms for all three tests are based upon the one-point-per-item scoring originally used with the *VMI.* All previous *VMI* scoring systems are still validly comparable.

This 4th Edition of the *VMI* Manual has been expanded to include the following:

• Updated reports of medical, neuropsychological, international, and other important advances in the use of the *VMI* in recent years.

• Standard scores at 2 and 4 month intervals for age 3 to adult and age norms for children as young as 28 weeks.

Authors

Keith Beery earned his doctorate in child development and clinical psychology at Purdue University. While at Purdue, he became deeply interested in helping children with learning difficulties as a result of studying with Newell Kephart. His internship at the Institute for Juvenile Research, a psychiatric child-guidance clinic in Chicago, confirmed his recognition of the importance of educational factors in child development.

After working with Barbara Bateman and Samuel Kirk at the University of Illinois in the newly developing field of learning disabilities, Keith worked in public schools to help establish early programs for children with learning and behavioral problems. He then became a member of the faculty in the Department of Pediatrics, at the University of California Medical School, San Francisco, and led multidisciplinary teams composed of educators, physicians, and other specialists working in clinics and in public schools.

Keith also has served as editor of the *Dimensions in Early Learning* monographs, director of the Institute for Independent Educational Research, director of Interstate Synergy, and board member of the National Inservice Network. His primary professional focus has been on the creation of educational environments that are supportive and growth-promoting for *all* of the children and adults who need to work well together.

Norman Buktenica designed 4 of the geometric forms which Keith's research selected for inclusion in the final 27-item version of the *VMI*. For many years Natasha Beery has helped to develop the *VMI*, and she has been instrumental in norming its supplemental *Visual* and *Motor* tests.

Acknowledgments

Beyond my wonderful family, I am most deeply indebted to the many beautiful children who have touched my life and have taught me most of what I know about learning and loving. Alfred and Valle Brokes, Joan McDonald, Secondo Sarpieri, Barbara Wander, Helene and Joe Wardlaw have proved to be especially good teachers. Many parents, teachers, specialists, administrators, professors, and researchers have taught and otherwise supported me. They know who they are and that I am eternally grateful to them.

The many fine teachers and others who administered, scored, or analyzed the *VMI* norming studies are too numerous to name here. But I thank them all, especially Rebecca Barcomb, Colleen, Mary Jo, Michael, and Natasha Beery, Penny D'Aleo, Jennella Crouch, Terry Fisher, Bette Goldstein, Sandy McEowen, Pam Miller, Chica Preda, Susan Queirolo, Scarlett Reader, Tracey Snites, Catherine Syversen, and Dyana Vukovich. Also, special thanks to the Australian Council for Educational Research, Rick Brownell, Mark Wilson, and Ben Wright for their statistical contributions to the *VMI* effort.

I very much respect and appreciate the excellent support and professionalism of the publishers and editors who have worked with me on behalf of children over the years with the *VMI*, in particular John and Anna Arena, Celia Argiriou, Dorothy Kirk, Arleta Quesada, and Bob Smith.

Among the pioneers who deserve major credit for the *VMI* are Barbara Bateman, Lauretta Bender, Grace Fernald, Arnold Gesell, Ruth Griffiths, Rhoda Kellogg, Newell Kephart, Samuel Kirk, Elizabeth Koppitz, Laura Lehtinen, Kurt Lewin, Jean Piaget, Alfred Strauss, Heinz Werner, and Max Wertheimer.

I. History and Perspective

During the author's internship with multidisciplinary teams in a psychiatric child-guidance clinic, he learned that children's abilities to copy geometric forms correlated significantly with their academic achievement. Correlations between some form-copying tests and readiness tests in kindergarten ranged from about .50 to .70 (107)[1]. Similarly, correlations between form copying and early reading achievement generally ranged from about .40 to .60 (113,142,150). Furthermore, neurologists, psychiatrists, and psychologists often based their diagnoses of emotional and neurological problems on how well children copied geometric forms. These diagnostic associations were being made on the basis of experience, on the work of Bender (19), Strauss and Kephart (172), and earlier Gestalt psychologists such as Werner (190) and Wertheimer (191).

Griffiths (70) and Kellogg (87) had extensively studied the spontaneous drawings of very young children. The abilities of children to copy a few of the more primitive forms, such as a circle and a square, had been well studied and documented by the Terman *Stanford-Binet* normings (174), Gesell (64), and others. Starr (170) had created a test that was useful for a limited age range.

The *Bender-Gestalt* (19) had been extensively used since 1938, but its forms were originally created by Wertheimer (191) for adult perceptual experiments, and the *Bender* had been used primarily with adults. Koppitz devised and normed a *Bender* scoring system for children and provided extensive summaries of research on its use (97,98).

Unfortunately, the effective scoring range on the Bender is only from about ages 5 to 9. Also, only two of the Wertheimer forms in the *Bender* have child-development characteristics adequate for inclusion in a developmental scale (8). Most importantly, the reliability and validity of the *Bender* are questionable (157).

---

[1]Numbers in parentheses are listed in the References section of this manual, pages 129-142.

Meanwhile, other investigators, the most noteworthy of whom were Birch (20), Bruner (28), Hunt (83), Piaget (138), and Vereecken (184), had developed educational theories and evidence to support a sensory-motor basis for development of intelligence and achievement. According to their work, higher levels of thinking and behavior require integration among sensory inputs and motor action. Kephart (88) in particular emphasized the importance of integration. A child can have well-developed visual and motor skills but be unable to integrate the two.

None of the form-copying tests at the time contained a sequence of forms, from less to more complex, that reflected normal development. Thus, in 1961, the *VMI* author began a series of experimental and empirical efforts to identify such a sequence of forms. A review of the rationale and outcomes of these studies was reported (8). After experimentation with many geometric forms and test formats with hundreds of children, a sequence of 24 forms, with a developmental age and distinct developmental characteristics, was established and normed in 1964 with Illinois children. The test was initially known as the *Developmental Form Sequence.* After further study, the test was published in 1967 as *The Beery-Buktenica Developmental Test of Visual-Motor Integration (VMI).*

Since 1967, the *VMI* has been extensively used in many countries and cultures for educational, medical, and other purposes (5,26,55,61,85,89,112,118,154,182,187,196). Further presentation of such studies will be made in Chapter VII. The *VMI* has been normed on several occasions since 1964, and rather consistent results have been obtained in the United States and elsewhere. At the preschool and elementary school age levels for which the *VMI* was primarily designed, the norms have been quite steady. The correlations among various normings and their scoring systems have been virtually perfect. For example, the correlation between 1-point and 4-point scoring was .98. Also, the *VMI* norms have been found to be appropriate for both group and individual administrations when the long-standing rule is followed to stop scoring after three consecutive forms have not been passed (38,144). Therefore, studies of the *VMI* made prior to 1996 are still relevant and are reported later in this manual.

It has been suggested that, since intelligence test scores appear to be increasing, perhaps *VMI* norms should also increase over time. The *VMI* has correlated moderately with intelligence tests, sharing, on average, about 25 percent of common variance with them. The two types of tests have some similarities, but are different. The *VMI* was designed to measure visual-motor integration, the coordination of visual and motor functioning, and to reflect developmental age differences in that arena. Thus, the *VMI* correlates far more with chronological age, .80 to .90, than with intelligence. The *VMI* appears to be a more sensitive index than global measures, such as intelligence, for at least some neuropsychological problems in child development (5). Physiologically, visual-motor integration appears to be mediated by at least some areas of the brain other than those for either general intelligence (154) or visual perception (67,152). The construct of visual-motor integration and its nervous system localization will be further discussed in Chapter II, and data supporting this construct are presented in Chapters VI and VII.

Are the testing and teaching assumptions that have sometimes been made about perceptual-motor tests valid? When the *VMI* was first created, many leading educators envisioned a great promise of help for children with disabilities by developing instruments to identify input-output modality strengths and weaknesses as a basis for remediation, or even prevention, of many learning and behavioral problems. These leaders and the *VMI* author hoped and tentatively assumed that adequate input-output functions, such as visual-motor integration, were (1) necessary prerequisites to success in school, (2) that when they were absent they should be remediated, and (3) that successful remediation of difficulties would enable students to be more successful. That vision has not come fully to fruition. However, in this author's opinion, the vision still holds promise in some areas, and we should not throw the baby out with the bath water. For example, insofar as the *VMI* is concerned, there is significant evidence of its predictive validity for some forms of school and other successes, as will be presented in Chapter VII. The basic concept of early intervention is solid, as attested by the excellent results, including *VMI* gains, in the Infant Health and Development Program (26).

Many would agree that Piaget and others have demonstrated considerable validity for a theory of sensory-motor bases for achievement. Although the differential value of modality-specific sensory-motor instruction is being questioned currently, aspects of the basic concept still hold considerable promise. As the research of Lyon and others (116) indicates, the psycholinguistic model can be quite useful for teaching.

During the 1960s and 1970s, however, many educators seemed to view visual-motor and other psycholinguistic abilities like muscles. If one simply exercised them by tracing circles, repeating digits, and so on, some thought that these abilities would become stronger and automatically transfer to academic and other tasks. It seems rather clear now that automatic transfer does not usually occur.

As this author has emphasized, transfer must be taught. For example, tracing circles and other geometric forms can be a valuable learning activity, depending upon an individual's present abilities and needs. But the learner must move on to tracing, copying, and writing the actual numerals, letters, and other specific stimuli involved in academic tasks, as outlined in Chapter VIII.

When this basic transfer principle is kept clearly in mind, the psycholinguistic model has considerable practical value. For example, Gerard and Junkala (62) demonstrated that handwriting improved markedly among children with learning disabilities when their teachers identified the children's input, associational, and output weaknesses and taught to these individual weaknesses, using *handwriting* stimuli. More such research is needed.

Several attempts to emulate the *VMI* have been made recently, but they have lacked quality and have been seriously flawed. The stimuli and tasks used in others' visual and motor subtests have differed significantly from those used in their visual-motor tests. For example, the placement of pegs into a pegboard is a motor task, to a great extent, but that task uses very different stimuli and motions than those used in the visual-motor task of copying geometric forms with a pencil. Use of disparate subtests to analyze components of a core test is a doubtful procedure. Combination of such subtests into a composite score is also questionable (76).

Another serious flaw in other visual-motor tests batteries is the claim that any one or all of their subtests can be given in any order desired. A basic fact in testing is that the *order* in which related tests are given often affects the scores. If, during norming, a set of subtests has been administered in a certain order, any change in that order can make field use of the norms inappropriate.

The *VMI* has grown with the times. In 1967, only age-equivalent norms were provided, which was a common practice with such tests at that time. Later, research revealed that age-equivalent norms are usually far less valid and appropriate than standardized scores, so the *VMI* was then provided with standardized scores. Weighted item scoring was provided in the 1989 *VMI* norming as a means to increase the sensitivity of the test to differences in the upper age ranges. The weighted scoring correlated almost perfectly (.98) with the original unweighted scoring and increased test sensitivity for older children. However, when the *VMI* supplemental tests for visual perception and motor coordination were introduced, the *VMI* was returned to the original unweighted scoring. Unweighted scoring is both easier and more valid for comparing performances on the supplemental tests to one another and to the *VMI* itself. Because previous *VMI* scoring systems have correlated so well with one another, and because even very different tests can be compared by means of their standard scores, 1997 *VMI* scoring system results can be validly compared with the results of all previous *VMI* scoring systems. Because young children tend to develop rapidly, norms for the *VMI* are now provided in 2-month intervals. Norms for the *VMI's* two supplemental tests are provided in 4-month intervals.

A number of important questions require further research regarding visual-motor development. Many children learn to compensate for visual-motor weaknesses by using other skills. At what price? For example, Rourke has reported that children's personalities are significantly affected by non-verbal learning disabilities (154). Would these children develop more fully and wholly, or at least more easily, if their visual-motor weaknesses were remediated? If so, how can such weakness best be remediated?

The efforts of everyone who has contributed to the *VMI's* development are greatly appreciated. Please continue to conduct studies and to otherwise let me know about the *VMI* 's strengths and needs so it can be made to serve children as well as possible.

Keith Beery

II. Rationale and Overview

This chapter provides (a) a rationale for the *VMI*, (b) a basic background in visual, motor, and visual-motor development, and (c) an overview of the *VMI* and its supplemental visual and motor tests.

> *From amoebas to humans and from infants to adults, successful development is characterized by increasing articulation and integration of parts with wholes.*

Rationale

The foregoing is an operating assumption that is based on Sherrington's work in biology and others in various fields of study, including the social sciences (204). In the broadest sense, this operating assumption is the *VMI*'s basic premise and purpose. Hopefully, a test of visual-motor integration can help some children to move forward toward more fully integrating all of their physical, intellectual, emotional, and spiritual parts with the whole of their selves and others.

More specifically, the primary purpose of the *VMI* is to help identify, through early screening, significant difficulties that some children have in integrating, or coordinating, their visual perceptual and motor (finger and hand movement) abilities. Through early identification, it is hoped that further difficulties can be prevented or remediated by appropriate educational, medical, or other interventions. It is not assumed that the appropriate intervention for all children who score poorly on the *VMI* is to have them draw circles, squares, and other forms. In fact, many children may be best helped by developing other modalities and/or learning processes, particularly if their visual-motor difficulties seem resistant to development. In some cases, it may be that *VMI* test results simply help to identify the need to bring services of various kinds to a child who appears to be at risk, which is another one of its important purposes. The *VMI* also may be useful in serving the purpose of evaluating the effectiveness of whatever educational, psychological, and/or medical services are provided. Additionally, it can serve a variety of purposes in educational, neuropsychological, and other forms of basic research.

Beyond its intended purposes, the construct, or what it is that the *VMI* attempts to measure and how well it measures that construct, needs to be defined. In order to do so, more background in visual, motor, and visual-motor development should be helpful.

Visual, Motor, and Visual-Motor Development

When the *VMI* was originally published in 1967, it was accompanied by a monograph, *Visual-Motor Integration*, which provided more detailed background in the phyletic (interspecies) and ontogenetic (human species) development of visual perception, motor coordination, and visual-motor integration than will be provided in the following pages (8). That monograph also reported upon the author's experimental work, such as children's estimations of angles. The following are brief developmental highlights, which are still valid today.

Visual Development

Phyletic All organisms are sensitive to light. Fairly high on the phylogenetic scale, some marine forms have paired pigment spots near the *brain*. At higher levels, pattern and size discrimination become possible. In some vertebrates, optic nerves completely cross to opposite sides of the brain. However, in mammals, the right half of each retina is connected to the right hemisphere of the brain and the left half of each retina is connected to the left hemisphere, an arrangement that probably contributes to the coordination of eye movements. In primates, the eyes are placed forward. This placement allows broad overlap between left and right visual fields. Thus, depth perception, convergence, and visual tracking are possible without moving the head. The result of this arrangement is binocular vision.

Ontogenetic The human eye develops out of the forebrain as early as the third week after fertilization. Babies born two months prematurely can differentiate light from darkness. By the fourth week, most babies can visually pursue a moving object.

Visual perception is probably best defined as the interpretation of visual stimuli, the intermediate step between simple visual sensation and cognition. Visual perception, therefore, is not visual acuity or sensation. Nor is it reading or other cognitive meanings. However, sensation, perception, and cognition probably all affect one another to varying degrees.

The Gestalt view that certain basic forms, such as the square, are *given* in perceptual experience is generally opposed today. Various combinations of light and dark boundaries are probably learned gradually and remembered to form percepts as the nervous system matures. As early as 28 weeks, most infants can learn to discriminate between a circle, cross, square, and triangle. (Other early developmental milestones are given on page 144.)

Part-whole integration has been of special significance in visual perceptual development (172). Parts of figure and ground must be differentiated and integrated with the whole. Many brain-injured persons seem able to analyze parts, but cannot synthesize the parts into wholes. Normal child development has been roughly outlined as follows: First, there is a focus on *wholes* (little attention to details) through age three. The focus then shifts to *parts* at ages four and five, to details by age six, and to integration of well-differentiated parts into wholes about age nine. These are rough *foci* of attention. Analysis and synthesis of parts and wholes is probably occurring at all ages.

Motor Development

Phyletic Many mammals possess manipulative ability, and the ability to grasp and move a variety of objects is well developed in primates. Thumb-finger opposition, which allows intricate and precise manipulation, is common among primates, and is most pronounced in humans.

Ontogenetic There is a developmental trend from generalized to specific activity. Mass action is followed by increased differentiation and subsequent integration of movement. Development also tends to progress in cephalo-caudal (from the head downward) and proximo-distal (spine outward) directions. Finger activity is the last ontogentic refinement of the shoulder-arm-hand complex. Spontaneous arm movements can be detected by the third fetal month. (Other such early developmental milestones are given on page 143.) Hand activity has been associated with cortical areas midway along the central fissure. The cerebellum seems to coordinate the actions of the various muscles involved in a specific act.

Visual-Motor Development

Phyletic From amoebas to humans, the nervous system seems to have progressed toward improved interaction among sensory and expressive modalities which were, in some cases, formerly separate. In adult humans, sensory and expressive modalities are usually well connected and coordinated, or integrated.

Ontogenetic Visual-motor may be the first sensory-response integration to develop. Kephart emphasized the importance of integration (88). He noted that a child could have well-developed visual and motor skills but be unable to integrate the two. Kephart speculated that integration might partly function subcortically, perhaps in the brainstem, somewhat akin to a telephone switchboard. If there were lack of development or damage in such areas, a visual-motor test might be sensitive to various kinds of integration problems, not only to visual-motor difficulties.

Vereeken reported that, in copying forms with a pencil, a child must first be visually aware of location and direction (184). This awareness is made possible through voluntary eye movement in a given direction. The child then proceeds to a constructive realization of this location through arm movements that correspond to the eye movements. Children can scribble vertical, horizontal, and circular lines before being able to imitate them, as scribbling requires little or no eye-hand coordination. Imitation is probably achieved before direct copying of these same forms because, in imitation, eye movements are rehearsed while the task is being demonstrated.

Vereeken reviewed Piaget's work on the development of spatial perception and reproduction (184). The earliest spatial level is *topological* and occurs during the first five years. During the topological period, neighborhood and separation, flatness or pointedness, continuity or discontinuity, and the containment or enclosure of one object by another are spatial attributes that are apprehended and reproduced. *Euclidean* spatial dimensions are usually achieved between ages five and ten. These include direction, rectilinear and curvilinear lines, lengths, and distances. *Projective* spatial achievement normally begins to develop during the euclidean period and progresses thereafter. At this stage an object can be seen in relation to other objects or from other points of view.

Finally, it is important to recognize that development may not always be smooth. Often, progress is in spurts and may even involve temporary regressions.

Keeping the foregoing and other development theories and research in mind, the *VMI* author set out to see if any existing form-copying tests were adequate and, if not, how a more adequate sequence of geometric forms could be developed.

Now, perhaps, would be a good time to articulate the *construct*, the *thing* that the *VMI* attempts to measure, and to consider how well it measures that construct. In doing so, some research will be briefly mentioned. A more detailed presentation is given in Chapters VI and VII.

> *Visual-motor integration is the degree to which visual perception and finger-hand movements are well coordinated.*

The *VMI* is designed to measure the hyphen in the term visual-motor integration on the premise that a whole can be greater than the sum of its parts, and that the parts may function well independently but not in combination.

Reliability A test can only be as valid as it is reliable. Thus, one would hypothesize that, if well constructed, the *VMI* will display acceptable internal, interjudge, and test-retest reliability. As detailed in Chapter VI, the *VMI* provides such reliabilities at high levels.

Validity In terms of validity, one would first hypothesize that the *VMI* should correlate well with chronological age. As shown in Chapter VII, the *VMI* measures up at very high levels, between .80 and .90. Secondly, one would hypothesize that the *VMI* should correlate at moderate levels, but not very high levels, with both good visual perceptual tests and with good motor coordination tests for the fingers and hands. One would also hypothesize that the *VMI* should correlate at relatively high levels with other tests that attempt to measure visual-motor integration. The foregoing relationships have been demonstrated and are detailed in Chapter VII.

The visual-motor integration construct implies that individuals with educational, psychological, and/or medical difficulties may have, on average, more difficulty with integration than their peers. Therefore, one would hypothesize that the *VMI* at least moderately differentiates such groups. As detailed in Chapter VII, overall, groups of children with various disabilities have performed less well on the *VMI* than their peers. The *VMI* has correlated highly with automatic-sequential integration tests with which many children with learning disorders have displayed the most difficulty. It was reported to be an effective measure for differentiating subtypes of reading disabilities. The *VMI* has correlated, often more significantly than other kinds of tests, with children's difficulties such as lead poisoning and low birth weight in various neuropsychological and medical studies.

Prediction Few perceptual-motor tests, besides the *VMI*, have offered evidence of their ability to predict academic or other problems. Generally, researchers have found the *VMI* to be a valuable predictor when used in combination with other measures. It has been reported to be a particularly good predictor of achievement by children from low socioeconomic groups. However, predictive correlations appear to decline as children move up the grade levels, presumably because academic demands upon visual-motor skills decline, relatively, and many children learn to compensate for visual-motor weaknesses by using other skills. The question still remains: Would these children achieve more fully and easily if their visual-motor weaknesses were remediated? And the related question remains: How can such weakness best be remediated?

What It is Not A very important means of defining something, like the construct of visual-motor integration, is to clarify what it is *not*. The *VMI* does not appear to be significantly related to gender, residence, or ethnicity, as detailed in Chapter VII.

Neuropsychological Localization

Where does visual-motor integration take place in the nervous system? Neuropsychologists generally ascribe visual-motor functions to the right hemisphere and to the motor cortex opposite the dominant hand (80). Grafton and others, on the basis of relative cerebral blood flow, concluded it unlikely that any single point in the brain would be responsible for *integrating* visual information into discrete motor plans. Rather, it seemed likely that this conversion occurred in both motor and sensory association areas, cerebellum and subcortical nuclei in a dynamic, parallel manner (67). Based to a great extent upon Halstead's (75), Luria's (115), and Reitan's (147) research, Rourke posits a model in which failures of development or disruption of various white matter neural connections seem likely to create visual-motor and/or other integrative disabilities in performance (154). These connections include those from right to left sides of the brain (the corpus callosum in particular), from front to back (especially for new tasks), and from top to bottom (cortex to brain stem). More localization research is needed.

Overview of the VMI and Its Supplemental Tests

The *VMI* and its two supplemental standardized tests, *Visual Perception* and *Motor Coordination*, provide the most valid and economical visual-motor screening battery available for preschool to adult ages.

The *VMI* is a developmental sequence of geometric forms to be copied with paper and pencil. The full, 27-item *VMI* can be either group or individually administered in about 10 to 15 minutes. A short, 18-item version is available for ages 3 to 7. First published in 1967, the *VMI* is used for and enjoyed by children throughout the United States and in other countries. Research indicates that the *VMI* is virtually culture-free. Because children with different backgrounds often have widely varying degrees of experience with alphabets and numbers, geometric forms are used in the *VMI* rather than letter or numeric forms.

The *VMI* is designed to assess the extent to which individuals can integrate their visual and motor abilities. If a child performs poorly on the *VMI*, it could be because he or she has adequate visual perceptual and/or motor coordination abilities, but has not yet learned to integrate, or coordinate, these two domains. Alternatively, it is possible that the child's visual and/or motor abilities are deficient. Therefore, examiners frequently follow up a *VMI* with an assessment of visual perceptual and motor abilities. This follow-up can be done with informal clinical evaluation, as outlined on pages 29-30. Or, if an examiner wishes to more formally and statistically compare a child's visual and motor abilities, the *VMI*'s new standardized supplemental tests can be administered. These standardized supplemental tests use the same stimulus forms as the *VMI*, whereas other existing visual-motor test batteries attempt to compare less related stimuli and tasks. All three tests were standardized on the same national

sample of 2,614 individuals and have established reliability and validity. Standard scores are provided at
frequent 2- and 4-month intervals.

Either one or both of the standardized supplemental tests
may be administered individually *after* the *VMI*. If all
three standardized tests are administered, they must be
administered in the same order in which they were
normed in order to yield valid results. The valid order of
administration is as follows: (1) *VMI*, (2) *Visual Perception,*
and (3) *Motor Coordination.* A statistical comparison of
results from the three tests can be quickly and easily made
on the graphic profile which is provided on the *VMI* test
booklets for this purpose. The three test results are not
averaged into one composite score, as in some batteries.
Composites of disparate measures are often meaningless.

In the standardized *Visual Perception* test, one geometric
form that is exactly the same as each stimulus is to be
chosen from among others that are not exactly the same as
the stimulus. During a three-minute period, the task is to
identify the exact match for as many of the 27 stimuli as
possible. In order to make this as pure a visual perceptual
task as possible, the motor requirements of the task are
reduced to a minimum by having the child simply point to
her or his choices. The stimuli on the *Visual Perception* test
were made smaller than those on the *VMI* test because a
very large and expensive test booklet would have been
required otherwise. Pilot tests of the stimuli were made
before norming and found to be satisfactory even for very
young children who did not have visual acuity problems.
Examiners should be alert for possible visual problems on
this and all other tests which require good near-point
visual acuity. Referral to the school nurse or to a vision
specialist should be made if there is reasonable doubt
about a child's visual status.

In the standardized *Motor Coordination* test, the task is to
simply trace the stimulus forms with a pencil without
going outside double-lined paths. Although visual
perception cannot be entirely eliminated in such motor
tasks, visual perceptual demands have been reduced
greatly by providing examples, starting dots, and paths as
strong visual guides for the required motor performance.
The *Motor Coordination* test takes about five minutes to
administer. Details of administration and scoring are
provided in Chapter III.

Uses of the VMI and its Supplemental Tests

The purposes of the *VMI* and its supplemental tests are to: (1) help identify significant difficulties in visual-motor integration, (2) obtain needed services for them, (3) assess the effectiveness of educational and other intervention programs, and (5) serve as a research tool. It is hoped that, through early screening with the *VMI*, those children who may need extra help in their educational or other aspects of development will be identified and referred to appropriate professionals for further evaluation and help.

Cautions

If a child's behavior during testing causes an examiner to suspect a visual acuity or other special problem, referral to a school nurse, an opthalmologist or other specialist may be indicated. No single test or score is sufficient for making a diagnosis or for creating a treatment plan. Team evaluation and planning is almost always best whenever possible.

Professional Requirements

For research, screening, and other purposes, the *VMI* and its supplemental tests can be administered and scored by almost any intelligent adult who is thoroughly familiar with the test materials and who has had supervised practice with an experienced examiner. However, for interpretation of test results, these tests require the educational background and experience of specialists in psychology, learning disabilities, or similar professions.

III. Administration and Scoring

The *VMI* can be validly administered as either a group screening test or for individual assessment purposes. Specialists often teach regular classroom teachers to administer the *VMI* as a class screening device, which simultaneously stimulates collaborative instructional and other planning.

Supplemental, standardized *Visual Perception* and *Motor Coordination* tests are provided as a means to statistically assess relative visual and motor contributions to *VMI* performance. Although the *Visual* and *Motor* tests have considerable potential for group testing, at present they are recommended for individual testing of those who have scored below the average range on the *VMI*.

It is not necessary to administer all three standardized tests in order to meaningfully assess visual, motor, and other factors that may affect *VMI* performance. In fact, *VMI* clinical "Testing the Limits" procedures (pages 29-30) are still strongly recommended for this purpose.

If the *Visual* and *Motor* tests are administered, it is extremely important that the sequence of testing is as follows: First the *VMI*, then the *Visual*, and then the *Motor*. As is true of many test batteries, exposure to one related test commonly affects performance on the next related tests. Therefore, norms can be seriously affected by changing the test order.

Norms may be invalid if the directions for administering tests are not followed or if the original testing materials are not used. These materials were carefully constructed to prevent glare, translucency, and other problems.

VMI Administration

The "Full" *VMI* Format, or booklet, is designed for ages 3 to adult. It contains all 24 *VMI* forms, including the initial 3 that are both imitated and copied directly, making a total of 27 items. The "Short" Format contains the initial 3 and the first 15 *VMI* forms, for a total of 18 items. The shorter format is designed for use with children age 3 to 7 years.

Usually, preschool children should be tested individually, using the individual instructions given on pages 27-29. Kindergartners often can be screened as an entire class if two or more adults monitor. Depending upon the class, it is sometimes best to test kindergartners in small groups of about 6 children. Children in first grade or above can be tested as an entire class. Older children can enter their own name, gender and birth date on the test booklet cover.

With all ages, monitor, encourage, and gently correct posture and procedural errors as needed.

Group Administration

1. Each child should have a sharpened No. 2 pencil, ideally without an eraser. A soft primary pencil or a ballpoint pen also are permissible.

2. Distribute the test booklets and say: *Please do not open your booklets until I ask you to do so. The page with the hand pointing up should face you.*

3. It is important that the booklets and each child's body be centered and squared with the desk during testing. As you demonstrate, say: *This is the way your booklet must stay on your desk until you are finished. This is the way you sit.*

4. As you demonstrate, say: *Now open your booklet by turning from the top, like this, to page 4. Page 2 has just blank squares on it, like this. Page 4 has forms in the top squares, like this.*

5. Demonstrate on the the chalkboard how to copy the forms, but do not use any of the test forms. Design your own forms. Say: *You are to copy what you see at the top of each page. Make your drawing of each form in the space below it, like this.*

6. Say: *Copy the forms in order. Start with item number 4. Numbers 1, 2, and 3 on the blank page are just for very young children.*

7. Say: *Some of the forms are very easy, and some are very hard even for adults.*

8. Say: *Do your best on both the easy and the hard ones; do not skip any.* (Repeat this phrase, as needed.)

9. Say: *Remember - only one try on each form and you cannot erase.*

10. Testing can be ended after all members of the group appear to have made 3 consecutive forms that do not earn points. Usually, 10 minutes suffice. If time and energy permit, however, you can allow everyone to try all of the forms. Those who finish early can draw, read, or engage in other activities of your choice.

Individual Administration

1. Many experienced examiners who plan to administer a variety of tests to an individual will usually begin with the *VMI* for two major reasons. *Rapport:* Almost all children enjoy doing the *VMI*, become absorbed in it, and feel successful. Typically, they like to try the harder items and want to do more. If not, that can be diagnostically significant. *VMI* time also is a quiet time to become comfortable with the examiner without having to use much verbal language. *Observation:* As the child draws, the examiner has a good opportunity to sit back and observe the child's attitude, body positions, movements, and other potentially important behaviors.

2. Some examiners remove the test booklet cover (pages 1, 2 ,15, and 16 on the Short Format; pages 1, 2, 23, and 24 on the Full Format) in order to record observations during the course of individual examinations, using page 15 on the Short Format or page 23 on the Full Format.

3. The child should have a sharp No. 2 pencil without an eraser, a primary pencil, or a ballpoint pen.

4. Place the test booklet face down in front of the child and squared to the child's desk or table.

5. Keep both the test booklet and the child's body centered and squared to the desk throughout testing. A different position of the booklet or the body can greatly affect the task.

6. Remember that imitated drawing of forms is typically much easier than direct copying. If the child is under 6 years of age or you anticipate a functional *VMI* level under 6 years of age, open the booklet to page 2 and say: *Watch me. I'm going to draw a line here.* If possible, sit beside the child. Then draw a vertical line approximately the same size, about two inches, as the one in box 4 on page 4. Point to the vertical line you just drew and then to the blank space below it. Say: *Make one like that. Make yours right here.* If the child does not respond successfully, make repetitive up and down vertical lines over your own first line. Then point to the child's space and say: *Do that. Make yours right here.*

7. Whether or not, after ample opportunity, the child draws vertical lines in imitation of yours, make repeated horizontal lines in the top-center box on page 2 and invite him to imitate you in the space below yours. Whether or not the child responds, repeat this procedure with circular lines at the top right-hand box on page 2. If the child succeeds on any one of these three imitation tasks, turn to page 4 and proceed as in instruction number 11 below.

8. If the child is 6 years of age or older and you do not anticipate a functional *VMI* level under 6 years of age, open the booklet to page 4, point to item 4 (the vertical line) and then to the blank space below it. Say: *Make one like that. Make yours right here.*

9. Encourage the child if necessary. Do not, however, trace the form with a finger or pencil, as such motions provide important cues. Do not let the child trace the form either. Avoid calling the form by its name or by a descriptive term.

10. If the child does not understand the direct copying task or does not copy any one of items 4, 5, or 6 well enough to earn a point on it, turn to the "blank" page 2 sheet and follow instructions 6 and 7 above.

11. If the child responds by imitating you on any one of the three imitation items, re-expose the first three printed forms, items 4 through 6, and allow the child to try again to copy the forms directly.

12. As many times as necessary, prompt by pointing to an item and saying: *Make one like this.*

13. Allow only one try per item, with no erasing. As soon as the child is responding well, say: *Good. Go ahead and do the rest of them. Turn to the next page when you finish this one.*

14. Say: *Do your best on both the easy and the hard ones; do not skip any.* (Repeat this phrase, as needed.)

15. Record your test observations inconspicuously. The child should not be timed overtly or otherwise pressured.

16. Testing may be ended after three consecutive items for which the child earns no points. You may wish to continue, though, as it is often informative to see how a child approaches more difficult items. Children usually enjoy copying and often ask to do even more forms.

Testing the Limits

Sattler (158) and others have suggested some excellent ways to informally assess the possible causes for a child's poor visual-motor integration performance and/or a child's potential for learning such skills. The following procedures are suggested.

Visual Perception After the regular *VMI* procedure has been completed, return to the first item on which the child did not meet the *VMI* scoring criteria. Ask the child to look at the stimulus and then at her or his attempted copy of the stimulus. Ask: *Does the form you drew look just the same as the one you copied?* (Pause for answer.) *How is it different?* Note whether or not the child perceives any differences that exist.

Motor Control Ask the child to *trace* the stimulus form with her or his pencil. Note the child's accuracy and ease in tracing.

Integration Ask the child to copy the stimulus form again on a blank sheet of paper. Note if the child's copy improved. If it improved, ask the child why he or she thinks it improved.

Imitation If the second try did not improve, sit next to the child and ask her or him to watch carefully as you copy the stimulus. Then give the child another opportunity to copy.

Motor Guidance If significant improvement has not been noted yet, hold and guide the child's hand and pencil while making another copy. Then let the child try again, unguided.

Examiner (Teacher) Verbalization If significant improvement still has not occurred, ask the child to watch and listen carefully as you recopy the stimulus and verbalize what you are doing, including your starting point(s), direction(s), and the key spatial relations that you monitor. Then ask the child to recopy the stimulus.

Child (Learner) Verbalization If significant improvement still has not been noted, ask the child to verbalize what you are doing as you copy the stimulus. Then ask the child to copy the stimulus while he or she verbalizes the actions.

Variations Develop and use variations of these suggested *teach and test* procedures that seem best suited to the individual's and your own examination needs.

Retention and Extension of Learning Using some or all of the foregoing procedures, consider teaching a child to adequately copy several or all of the *VMI* forms on which he or she did not meet criteria on your first examination. About two weeks later, repeat the regular *VMI* procedure with the child to see how well learning has been retained and/or extended to other stimuli.

This retention check often reveals which children are simply *inexperienced* in visual-motor integration efforts. These children tend to retain what you have taught. Other children will display the *leaky bucket* syndrome characteristic of many children with learning disabilities. These children tend not to retain or extend visual-motor integration learnings unless they are provided with clear cognitive supports, such as rules about how to proceed, and/or extensive rote practice and review.

VMI Scoring

Scoring of the *VMI* is now basically the same as it it was in the 1989 manual edition, with two important differences:

1. One-Point Scoring: As was true prior to 1989, only one point per *VMI* form is now given in order to facilitate as direct comparison as possible between the *VMI* and the supplemental Visual and Motor tests. The 1989 weighted scoring (1 to 4 points per form) correlated almost perfectly (.98) with the current one-point scoring, which was used in all editions prior to 1989.

2. 27 Total Points: In 1996 scoring, imitated drawings of the first three forms (the vertical line, the horizontal line, and the circle) are included in the total score and standardized norms. Thus, there are now 27 possible raw score points.

One of the beauties of standard scores is that they enable appropriate statistical comparisons between different tests, including test results from the 1997 and all previous editions of the VMI.

Imitated and Copied Forms The scoring criteria for both imitated and copied forms are exactly the same. Only the age equivalents differ, as shown on the following reduction of the Recording and Scoring sheet which appears on the inside cover of the *VMI* test booklet:

					VMI Recording and Scoring					
No.	Form	Age Norm (Yrs-Mons)	Score	Observations		No.	Form	Age Norm (Yrs-Mons)	Score	Observations
1		2-0 Imitated				14		5-9		
2		2-6 Imitated				15		6-5		
3		2-9 Imitated				16		6-8		
4		2-10 Copied				17		7-5		
5		3-0 Copied				18		7-11		
6		3-0 Copied				19		8-1		
7		4-1				20		8-11		
8		4-4				21		9-6		
9		4-6				22		10-2		
10		4-7				23		10-11		
11		4-11				24		11-2		
12		5-3				25		12-8		
13		5-6				26		13-2		
	VMI Raw Score = total points scored up to 3 consecutive No Scores. Record raw score on front page. See the 1997 VMI Manual for norms. Copyright © 1997 by Keith E. Beery and Norman A. Buktenica.					27		13-8		

31

The Recording and Scoring sheet lists the "Norm Age" for each form, the age at which about 50 percent of children meet the developmental criteria for a given form. Many examiners use this sheet to help parents better understand their child's current level of development.

Criteria *VMI* scoring is based upon the *Score* and *No Score* criteria and examples shown for each of the 24 forms on pages 34-81. The criteria and examples were derived from careful study of each form's developmental evolution, based upon thousands of children's reproductions. Developmental comments and trend illustrations for the forms will be found on pages facing the scoring criterion pages.

Experienced scorers will find the Summary Scoring display on pages 82-83 useful as a reminder of the basic scoring criteria.

Protractor A number of the criterion pages contain illustrations for using a protractor. All protractor degrees are read clockwise with the base of the protractor on the horizontal. These illustrations are intended as aids for learning how to score the *VMI* because they have been effective for this purpose in university and other settings. The author is particularly indebted to Lepkin & Pryzwansky (106) for their research in this regard.

Most experienced scorers will seldom need a protractor or ruler in scoring the *VMI*. In fact, a major rule to remember in scoring a form is: *If in doubt, score it as meeting the criteria.* Some scorers tend to be too strict. In general, it is better to gain a good developmental sense or *gestalt* for each form's evolution by carefully studying its developmental trends than it is to overly focus upon the details of reproduction.

Exceptions An experienced examiner will develop a *gestalt* of a given child's developmental behavior on the *VMI*. For example, it is common to encounter an older child who somewhat hastily copies the easier forms, not bothering to *dot the i's and cross the t's*, as the forms are well within the child's command. An experienced examiner takes such behaviors into account in scoring.

Occasionally, a child makes a second attempt at a form. Always score the first attempt of children below age 9. If you did not actually see which was first, it often can be identified by comparing the sizes of dual attempts relative to the sizes of the child's single attempts on other forms.

Accept productions of children over age 9 who first sketch with light lines, then complete a form with darker lines.

Basal The imitated forms on page 2 of the *VMI* test booklet are not administered during group testing or to most children over six years of age during individual testing. As with any test's basal, assume that the imitated forms would have been drawn adequately if a child succeeds with the more difficult task of direct copy on Forms 4, 5, and 6. If any of Forms 4, 5, or 6 are not passed, the imitated forms should be administered and scored.

Ceiling Although you may continue testing beyond a child's current ability level, stop *scoring* after 3 consecutive forms have not been passed. This basic rule applies whether individual or group administration of the *VMI* is used, and whether or not a child attempted more forms after 3 consecutive forms were not passed.

Short Form Administration, scoring and norm table use are the *same* for both the short, 18-item and the full, 27-item booklet versions of the VMI. The short, 18-item version should not be used with children older than 8 years and 0 months of age.

Scoring Criteria

Age Norms: 2-0 Imitated
2-10 Copied

1. Over 1/2 of line(s) within 30° of vertical

Score 1	No Score

Supplemental Information

The same scoring criteria are used for both imitated and copied lines. See pages 25-30 for differences in test administration.

Imitated Vertical Line   Age Norms

Gesell (63): 40% at age 1-6 and 79% at age 2-0 succeed 1-9
Gesell (64) 2-0
Griffiths (70) 2-0
Cattell (32) 2-3
Stanford-Binet (LM) 3-0

The above norms are based on the child's reproduction of a *single* vertical stroke. However, on the *VMI*, repeated vertically oriented lines by the examiner and child are also acceptable. An age norm of 2-0 has been estimated for *VMI* imitation. The greater freedom allowed by the *VMI* on this form has been effective in eliciting responses from young or shy children.

Copied Vertical Line

Based upon 1996 standardization data, the age norm for copying is 2-10.

Age Norms: 2-6 Imitated
3-0 Copied

Scoring Criteria

1. Over 1/2 of line(s) within 30° of horizontal

Score 1	No Score

Supplemental Information

Imitated Horizontal Line

Age Norms

Griffiths (70): horizontal scribbles 1-8
Griffiths (70) horizontal stroke 2-0
Gesell (63): 41% at age 2-0 and 95% at age 3-0 succeed 2-6
Gesell (64) 2-6
Cattell (32) 2-6

It is difficult to disregard Griffith's data, but imitation of horizontal lines, as opposed to spontaneous horizontal scribbling at 2-0, has seldom been observed by the *VMI* author.

Copied Horizontal Line

It is fairly common for children younger than 3-0 to make vertical lines while attempting to copy a horizontal line. The reverse, making horizontal lines while attempting to copy a vertical line, is less common. These findings are further evidence that the horizontal line is more difficult to make than the vertical.

Scoring Criteria

Age Norms: 2-9 Imitated
3-0 Copied

1. Any loop with a ratio of no more than 2 to 1 between its height and width

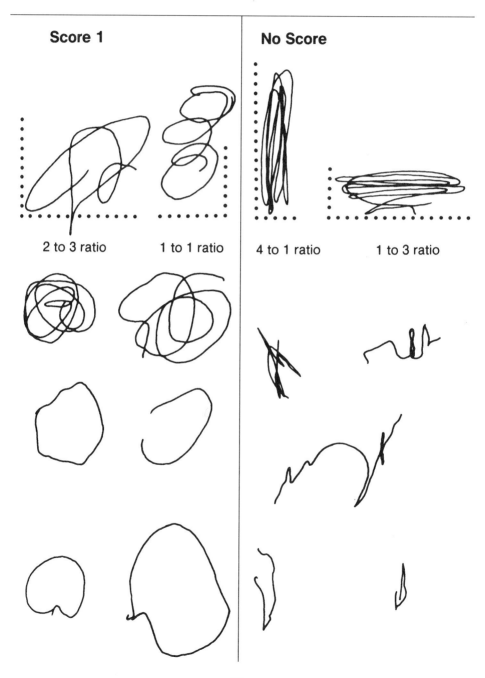

| Score 1 | No Score |

2 to 3 ratio   1 to 1 ratio   4 to 1 ratio   1 to 3 ratio

Supplemental Information

Imitated Circle   Age Norms

Griffiths (70): circular scribble 1-11
Gesell (63): 59% at age 2-0 and 86% at age 3-0 succeed 2-0
Gesell (64) 2-0
Cattell (32) 2-6

Most experience indicates that this task is performed quite early. However, data gathered for this study suggest an age estimate of 2-9 for the *VMI* imitated circle.

Copied Circle   Age Norms

Gesell (63) 3-0
Gesell (64) 3-0
Stanford-Binet (LM) 3-0
Merrill-Palmer 3-3
Bayley (7) 3-4

The *VMI* estimate of 3-0 for the copied circle is in agreement with the results of other investigators.

Children under age 6-0 tend to begin a circle at the bottom (i.e., near their bodies) and to draw away from themselves, a behavior that is compatible with their typical perception that they are at the very center of the universe. Directionality is basically perceived as either *away from me* or *toward me* rather than in terms of right, left, up, or down. The child's right-left center seems to be the forehead. Children over age 6-0 usually begin near the top of the circle and make the initial movements toward their bodies.

Contrary to common belief, children between ages 3-0 and 6-0 tend to make smaller circles than do other children. However, the reproductions of older children are more accurate in size.

FORM 7 Vertical-Horizontal Cross

Age Norm: 4-1

Scoring Criteria

1. Two intersecting lines

   not:

2. All 4 "legs" at least 1/4" long (not including extensions)

   not:

3. At least 1/2 of each line within 20° of correct angle

   not:

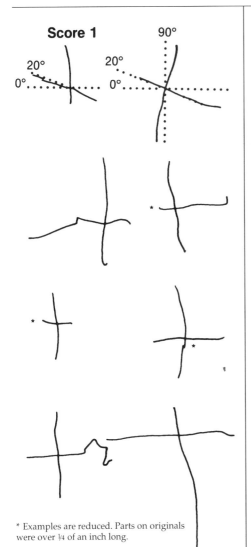

Score 1

90°

20°

20°

0°

0°

No Score

25°

25°

3

2**

1

3

1

2*

3

2

3

3

3

3

1

3

* Examples are reduced. Parts on originals were over ¼ of an inch long.

** Numerals refer to scoring criteria listed at the top of the page.

40

Supplemental Information

Imitated Cross   Age Norms

Gesell (63): 3% at age 2-0 and 77% at age 3-0 succeed 2-10
Gesell (64) 3-0

The author has done no systematic work with the imitated cross but
considers 3-0 too low an estimate for the task. 3-3 is probably closer.

Copied Cross   Age Norms

Gesell (63): 55% at age 4-0 and 53 % at age 5-0 succeed 4-0
Gesell (64) 4-0
Merrill-Palmer (1948) 4-6

Successful achievement of this form is primarily dependent on the child's
ability to cross the vertical line with a *continuous* horizontal line. There is
some evidence to indicate the following developmental pattern:

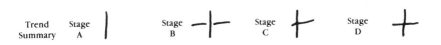

Reproductions of this form by children up to age 4-6 commonly display a
bold vertical line and a weak horizontal line. Segmenting (Stage B) is
definitely an immature trait occurring most often in the horizontal line. It
is thought that this fact is related to the phenomenon that Kephart (88)
refers to as *crossing the midline*. With reference to the spine as the midline
of the body, children have difficulty in making a smooth movement
across the midline, probably because they have to *reverse* at that point
from a *toward me* motion to an *away from me* motion. The difficulty is
usually observed in activities on a large spatial scale such as chalkboard
work, but may occur with young children even in pencil work. Reading
and writing reversals are often based on midline problems at older ages.

Consistent with Kephart's discussion of the problem, the author has
observed that a child who segments the horizontal line often draws the
left segment from left to right and the right segment from right to left (or
the reverse combination).

Vereecken (184) reported that a child who segments the horizontal line
will draw to the midline and stop, even after the examiner has manually
guided the child's hand through the midline several times. He further
noted that the ability to make vertical structures with blocks precedes
that of making similar horizontal structures.

FORM 8 Right Oblique Line

Age Norm: 4-4

Scoring Criteria

1. A "single" line (extensions OK)   not:

2. At least 1/2 of the line within 110°-160°   not:

3. No *abrupt* change of direction   not:

Score 1	**No Score**
	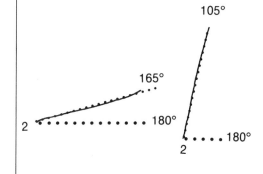

Supplemental Information

Copied Right Oblique Line

Vereecken (184) cited a report that the right oblique line was not reproduced until 5-6 to 6 years of age and that the left oblique line was not reproduced until 6 to 6-6 years of age. Vereecken found, however, that many 5-year-olds could perform these tasks. Bender (19) suggested that oblique lines were not copied correctly until age 9 or 10.

There seems to be little question that the obliques develop later than the vertical and horizontal lines and that the right oblique precedes the left oblique, at least for right-handed persons. However, the more extensive VMI data do not support earlier estimates concerning the age levels at which oblique lines are accomplished.

The present data suggest the following developmental progression in the achievement of oblique lines:

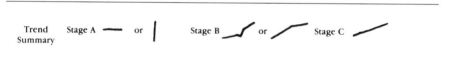

Most early errors consist of horizontal straight lines. Vereecken (184) pointed out that execution of the oblique lines requires the *simultaneous* coordination of vertical and horizontal movement. Most near successes show evidence of difficulty with such coordination, with excursions into simple vertical or horizontal movements, as in Stage B above. Children can perceive obliqueness and have the motor ability to execute oblique lines long before they can reproduce them.

Crossing the midline may be the basis for some Stage B productions. This can be checked by having the child copy oblique lines to the right and the left of the midline. At older ages, moving a child's book to the left and/or right sometimes reduces reversals while the child is being taught to cross the midline easily.

FORM 9 Square

Scoring Criteria

Four clearly defined sides (corners need not be angular) not: ⊃ ◯

Score 1

No Score

Supplemental Information

Copied Square   Age Norms

Stanford-Binet (L, LM) 4-0
Gesell (64) 4-6
Gesell (63): 53% at age 5-0 succeed 5-0

In most evaluations of pencil copies of the square, attention is focused on the corners of the reproduction. There are good reasons for this, as the square is usually the first form presented to children that requires them to draw in one direction, stop the line in a fairly specific area, and then continue in a different direction. Kephart (88) recognized the importance of this ability to stop and change direction and noted that its absence is often associated with pathology in older children. However, deviations in corners of the square occur too frequently throughout the age range of the present sample for the author to regard them as criteria for success on the form. It appears that most children are at least 6 years old before they can produce four good corners. Actually, diamonds appear to be more informative of *stop-and-go* ability, inasmuch as both obtuse and acute turns are required.

Four-sidedness seems to be the better criterion for success on the square. Empirically, this criterion provides the simplest and most reliable basis for scoring. The author's experience supports Vereecken's (184) argument that the perception of spatial relationships among the *sides* of the square is closely related to achievement on this form. The following developmental trend supports this argument:

Trend Summary	Stage A	Stage B	Stage C	Stage D

Some children copy a square in the following fashion: ⬭. Such constructions indicate that these children have *seen* the corners and realize something should be done about them. However, despite the ability to perceive and to reproduce the straight vertical and horizontal lines of which the square is composed, they have not been able to organize these components. If they had been able to do so, they would have at least drawn something like this: ⊏⊐ . Children who organize the lines in such a manner nearly always go on to complete four corners: ⊔ .

FORM 10 Left Oblique Line

Scoring Criteria

1. A "single" line (extensions OK)   not:

2. At least 1/2 of the line within 20°-70°   not:

3. No *abrupt* change of direction   not:

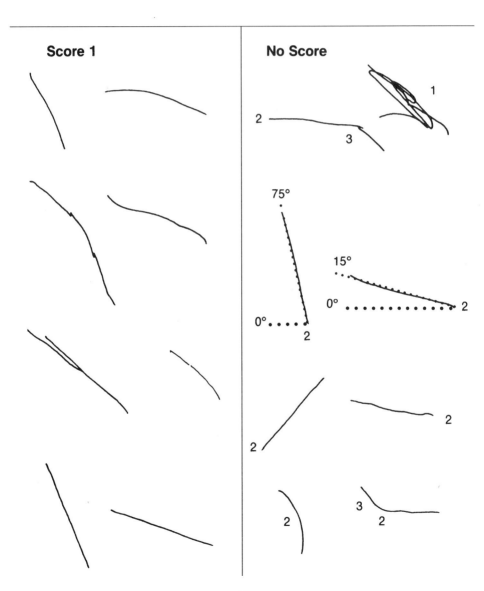

Score 1

No Score

1

2

3

75°

0°

2

15°

0°

2

2

2

3

2

2

Supplemental Information

It was mentioned earlier that reproduction of the right oblique line usually occurs earlier than that of the left oblique line, by some estimates, a full year earlier. (See the general discussion of obliques accompanying Form 8.) However, this applies more to right-handed than to left-handed individuals. Furthermore, the age difference in performance is debatable. The author's data indicate that the left oblique is executed, on average, within 3 to 6 months after the right oblique. This difference may be attributed to mechanical difficulties rather than to perceptual differences.

Right-handed persons usually have a complete view of the reproduction in constructing the right oblique. In reproducing the left oblique, however, right-handed persons cannot see where to aim the line because their hands and wrists obstruct their view.

FORM 11 Oblique Cross

Scoring Criteria

1. Two intersecting lines

2. Lines angles between 20°-70° and 110°-160°

3. Longest of 4 unextended legs no more than twice as long as shortest (not including extensions)

not:

not:

not:

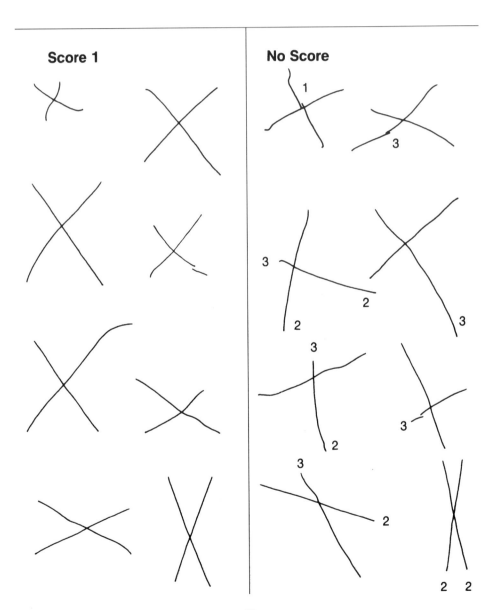

Supplemental Information

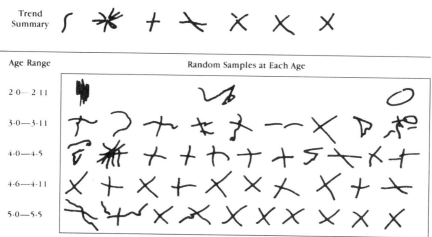

Age Range	Random Samples at Each Age
2·0 — 2·11	
3·0 — 3·11	
4·0 — 4·5	
4·6 — 4·11	
5·0 — 5·5	

Imitated Cross

Age Norm

Stanford-Binet (M) 3-6

The imitated oblique cross may fill the age gap between the copied circle and the copied vertical-horizontal cross. The examiner who wants the child to imitate the oblique cross should wait until the child has completed the *VMI*.

Copied Cross

Some of the developmental phenomena observed in earlier forms appear here:

1. Vertical and horizontal lines are drawn prior to oblique lines.

2. The right oblique is reproduced before the left oblique.

3. There is difficulty in crossing the midline.

Note that both obliques may require crossing the midline. Segmenting of either or both lines is commonly found in early attempts.

FORM 12 Triangle

Scoring Criteria

1. Three clearly defined sides   not:

2. One corner higher than others   not:

Score 1	**No Score**

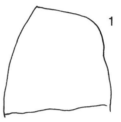 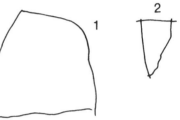

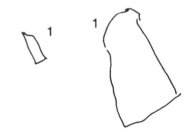

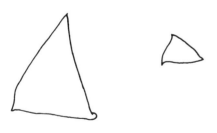

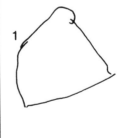 

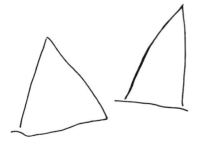

Supplemental Information

Age Range	Random Samples at Each Age
2·0—2·11	
3·0—3·11	
4·0—4·5	
4·6—4·11	
5·0—5·5	
6·0—6·3	
7·0—7·3	
8·0—8·3	

Copied Triangle

Age Norms

Gesell (63): 40% at age 5-0 and 95% at age 6-0 succeed 5-3
Gesell (64) 5-0

This form emerges rather suddenly. As in the square, circularity is the main tendency the child must overcome. However, the problem is more difficult in the case of the triangle because oblique lines must be coordinated.

Note the consistency with which vertical-horizontal forms precede similar oblique forms: $|-$ vs. $/\backslash$, $+$ vs. $\times$, and $\square$ vs. $\triangle$.

Note also that the closed forms follow similar open forms: $+$ vs. $\square$ and $\times$ vs. $\triangle$.

It is highly unusual for the base line of the triangle to depart more than a few degrees from the horizontal after the age of 7-0.

FORM 13 Open Square and Circle

Scoring Criteria

1. No more than 1/16" separation or overlap of forms   not:

2. No major distortions of circle or open square   not:

3. Height of circle and square within a 2 to 1 ratio   not:

4. Bisector of circle passing through corner of square must project *into* the square   not:

Score 1	**No Score**

	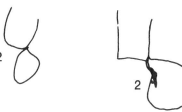

*Examples reduced. Gap on original was over 1/16".

Supplemental Information

Trend Summary	

Age Range	Random Samples at Each Age
2-0—2-11	
3-0—3-11	
4-0—4-5	
4-6—4-11	
5-0—5-5	
5-6—5-11	

Although developmental stages of this form are difficult to determine, it should be noted that placement of the circle at the lower right corner of the open square usually does not occur before age 5-0.

This form is one of several in the sequence that seems to magnify visual-motor difficulties. Failures are usually obvious. Even the illustrations of No Scores on the opposite page do not fully reflect the degree of distortion that is characteristic of children below age 5-0 or of older children who have visual-motor problems.

FORM 14 Three-Line Cross

Age Norm: 5-9

Scoring Criteria

1. Three intersecting lines

not:

2. Intersection gap no more than 1/8" in height

not:

3. Over 1/2 of horizontal line within 15° correct

not:

4. Over 1/2 of both diagonals more than 10° from vertical

not:

Score 1	**No Score**
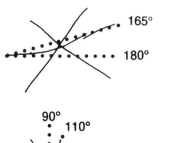	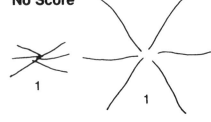
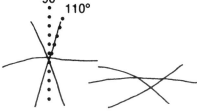	
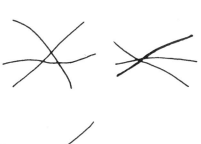	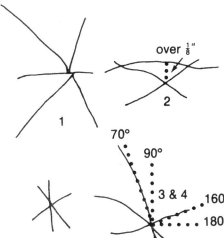
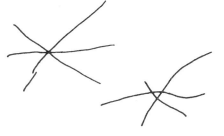	

Supplemental Information

Trend Summary								

Age Range	Random Samples at Each Age

Form 14 differs from the Merrill-Palmer form (age norm: 5-0), which has equal angles between all lines. However, immature subjects tend to draw horizontal lines in both cases.

Form 14 is more subject to segmentation at the midpoint than any of the other crossing forms. See Kephart (88) regarding the midline problem. Note that children may shift their bodies to the left or right of the stimulus to avoid the problem. Shifting should not be allowed during VMI testing.

One will find reproductions that display obtuse upper and lower angles scattered throughout the age range 5-0 through 11-11. However, it is not until about 13-0 that this dimension appears with consistency. These latter reproductions are characterized by a greater obtuseness of the appropriate angles than exists in the stimulus. In general, exaggerations of this kind are found beyond the age level at which a form dimension is achieved. Usually the child is merely emphasizing awareness of the dimension.

FORM 15 Directional Arrows

Age Norm: 6-5

Scoring Criteria

1. Absence of reversed or "floating" tips (see page 57 notes)   not:

2. Sharp points on tips   not:

3. No directional confusion   not:

4. Longest of 4 legs no more than twice as long as shortest   not:

Score 1	**No Score**
 	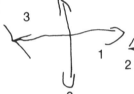

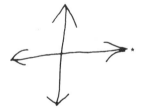	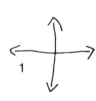 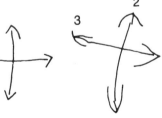
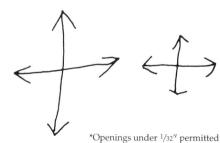	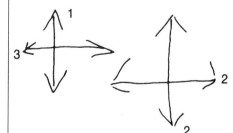

*Openings under 1/32" permitted

56

Supplemental Information

Trend
Summary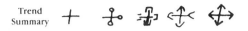

Age	Developmental Trends	Random Samples at Each Age
2-0	No response	
3-0	Vertical-horizontal lines	
4-0	Some indications of points	
4-4	Points at all ends	
4-6	V-shaped points developing	
5-6	Better control of points	
6-5	Adequate control	

The fact that the points, if extended, would form the sides of a tilted square is realized by only a few children, even in the older age groups. The points are usually more acute in the reproductions than they are in the stimulus, where they are 90° angles.

This form is particularly valuable as an indicator of a young child's developing directionality. However, it presents a bit of a scoring problem for older children, who tend to copy it quickly because it is within their easy command. *Floating* points among these children are fairly common as a result. Therefore, allow floating points of no more than 1/16 of an inch if the reproduction is otherwise good and the child succeeds on each of the next three forms.

FORM 16 Two-Dimensional Rings

Scoring Criteria

1. Three overlapping circles showing seven openings
   The triangular opening in the center must show.

2. One circle clearly below the others (Position can be checked by connecting the mid-points of the circles to form a triangle. The lowest side of the triangle must be 20° or more off horizontal.)

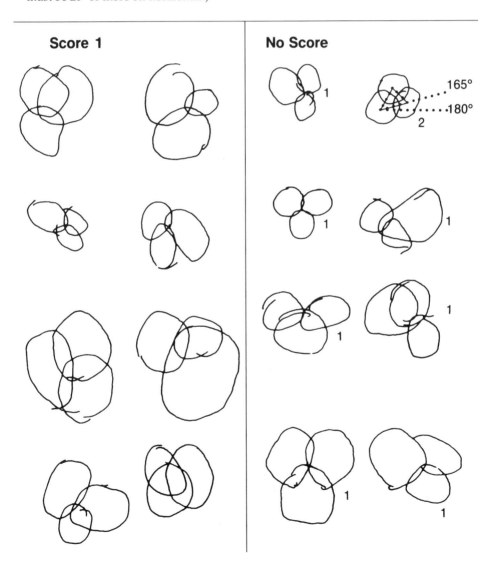

Score 1	No Score

Supplemental Information

Age	Developmental Trends	Random Samples At Each Age
3-0	Minimal response	
3-10	Groups of circles	
4-6	Two or more linked	
5-0	Better grouping	
6-0	General positioning, but incomplete overlap	
6-8	Essential reproduction	
8-0	Fairly rounded and balanced	

No essential change is noted beyond age 8-0.

FORM 17 Six-Circle Triangle

Scoring Criteria

Age Norm: 7-5

1. Six circles   not:

2. Baseline and at least one other side straight   not:
   (Dotted line must at least touch the edge of
   each circle.)

3. Baseline within 10° of horizontal   not:

4. Space between circles on the *same* side no more than 2 to 1   not:

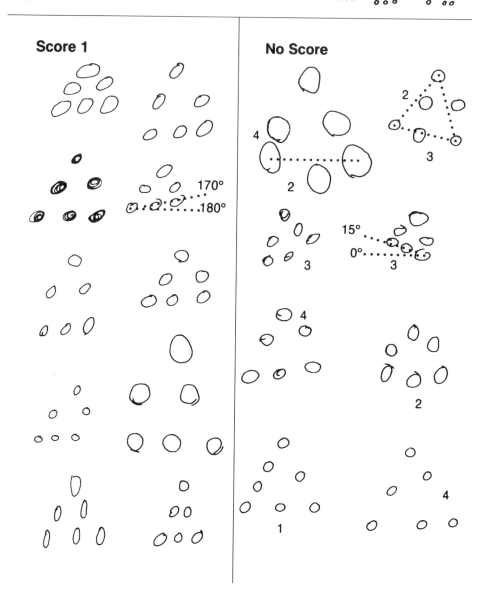

Score 1   **No Score**

Supplemental Information

Trend Summary

Age	Developmental Trends	Random Samples at Each Age
3-0	Little or no response	
4-0	Two or more circles	
4-6	Closed form emerging	
5-4	Closed form, rounded or curved	
6-0	Triangularity emerging	
7-5	Two straight sides	
12-0	Precise circles and placements	

Rounded sides are the major scoring aspect, as it is clearly an immature tendency. Precise placement is usually achieved by constructing the corner circles first and then inserting the remaining circles midway between the corners.

FORM 18 Circle and Tilted Square

Scoring Criteria

1. Four-*cornered* square and a circle   not:

2. Opposite corners within 10° of vertical and horizontal   not:

3. Square "touches" circle with *closed* corner   not:

4. No more than 1/16" gap or overlap of forms   not:

5. Contact of corner within middle 1/3 or circle   not:

6. Heights of circle and square not more than 2 to 1 ratio   not:

Score 1	No Score

Score 1

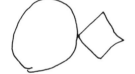

No Score

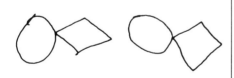

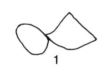
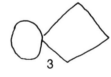

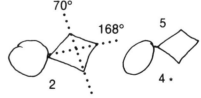

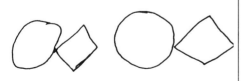

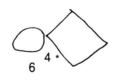

* Examples reduced
Originals over 1/16"

Supplemental Information

Age	Developmental Trends	Random Samples at Each Age
3-0		
4-0	One or two circular forms	
4-6	Two closed forms; one angular	
5-0	Square on horizontal plane	
5-8	Square tilted, usually separated	
6-4	Imbalanced, but close	
7-11	Balanced, touches at median of circle	

Form 18 is one of the best illustrations in the sequence of Werner's concept of hierarchical integration (190). The first example above for age 5-0 may appear to be a better reproduction than the last example at age 5-8 or the third example at age 6-4. However, the older child has attempted to add a dimension (tilting the square) that the younger child has not. Until the added dimension is integrated, the reproductions are not as neat as the 5-0 example, which is integrated at a lower level. The two parts are often separated by the child who is attempting to integrate a new dimension. On this form and others, however, separation of component parts may indicate a generalized difficulty in integrating parts into a cohesive whole. In the latter case, separation occurs even in forms that the child has otherwise mastered.

Like Form 13, this form seems to magnify visual-motor disabilities in children. Distortions for such children are apt to be gross.

FORM 19 Vertical Diamond

Age Norm: 8-1

Scoring Criteria

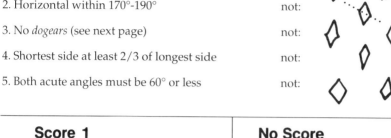

1. Four good corners (openings under 1/16")   not:

2. Horizontal within 170°-190°   not:

3. No *dogears* (see next page)   not:

4. Shortest side at least 2/3 of longest side   not:

5. Both acute angles must be 60° or less   not:

Score 1   No Score

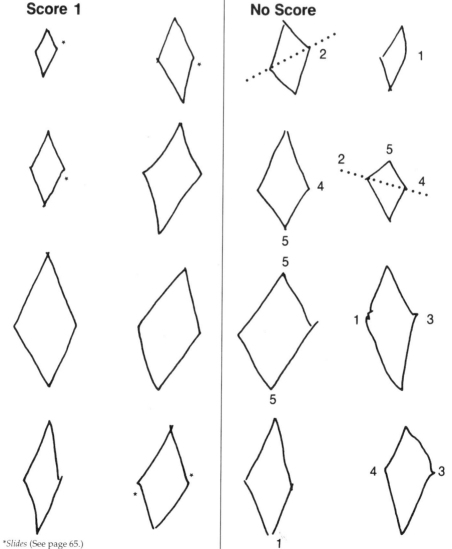

Slides (See page 65.)

Supplemental Information

Age	Developmental Trends	Random Samples at Each Age
3-0	Vertical lines	
4-0	Reflections of vertical and straight lines	
5-0	Closed form with angles	
5-8	Squared	
6-10	Definitely elongated	
8-1	Acceptable angularity	

In the *Stanford-Binet (LM)*, the vertical diamond was regarded as a 7-0 task. It should be noted that the top and bottom angles (45°) of Form 19 are more acute than are those of the Binet diamond. It is the relatively accurate representation of these 45° angles that is the major criterion on Form 19. As shown above, the immature tendency is to make acute angles too large.

Dogearing is a behavior that deserves notice. The immature child has difficulty in turning a corner; the dogear introduces an extra line and an extra angle to the form. The mature child (often in a hurry to complete a form well within his or her ability) may *slide* in and out of a corner, thereby introducing a slight curve to the lines near the point, but does not add extra lines and angles. This behavior is not penalized unless it is extreme.

Immature (Dogeared)   Mature (Curved)

FORM 20 Tilted Triangles

Scoring Criteria

Age Norm: 8-11

1. Two triangles   not:

2. Two corners of inner triangle cleanly touch middle 1/3 of outer triangle sides. Third corner within 1/16" of cleanly touching (may either under- or over-lap).   not:

3. Left outer angle within 60°-120°   not:

4. Right outer side slopes 100° or more   not:

Score 1   **No Score**

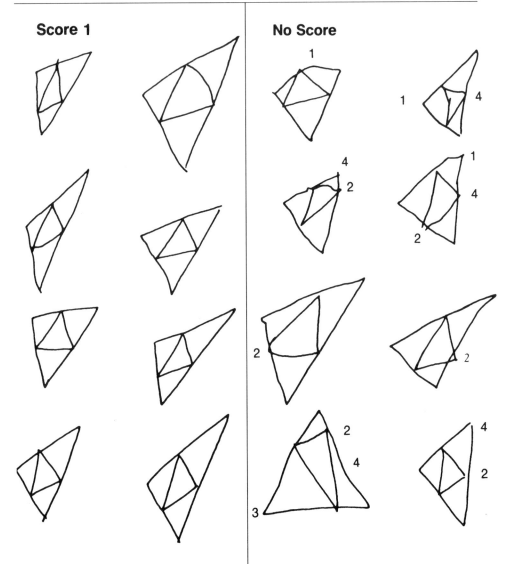

66

Supplemental Information

Age	Developmental Trends	Random Samples at Each Age
4-0	Single, closed form	
5-0	Enclosed form that floats	
6-0	Two triangles; one or more corners touching sides	
7-6	All corners touch or overlap.	
8-11	Acceptable	
10-0	Little change	
12-0	Slope and elongation are integrated.	

The immature tendency is to produce a floating inner form.

The correct slope of the form and accurate representation of the 90° angle of the outer triangle are observed prior to age 8-0. However, these two factors are seldom coordinated before age 8-7.

The hypotenuse of the outer triangle is usually too short until the child is 12 years old, but this variable did not prove reliable enough to be included in the criteria.

FORM 21 Eight-Dot Circle

Scoring Criteria

1. Eight dots, circles, or dashes

   not:

2. Circularity: no 3 adjacent dots fall on a straight line

   not:

3. Spacing: Greatest space between any two dots no more than twice the shortest space

   not:

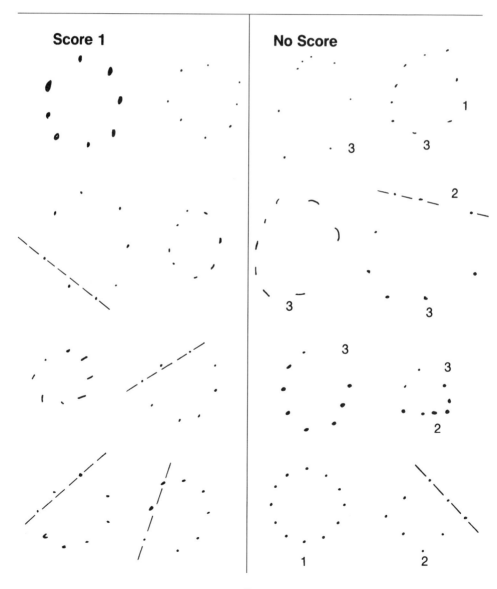

Score 1

No Score

Supplemental Information

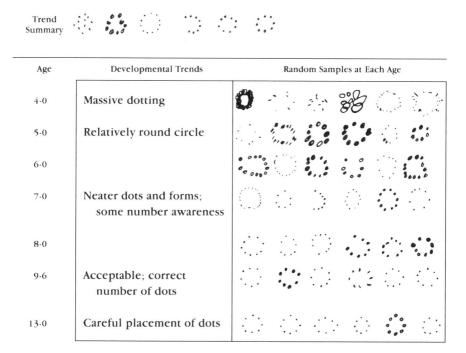

Age	Developmental Trends	Random Samples at Each Age
4-0	Massive dotting	
5-0	Relatively round circle	
6-0		
7-0	Neater dots and forms; some number awareness	
8-0		
9-6	Acceptable; correct number of dots	
13-0	Careful placement of dots	

Many children make clean, circular dots from age 8 through 15. Large, filled-in dots are common between ages 5 and 8.

FORM 22 Wertheimer's Hexagons

Age Norm: 10-2

Scoring Criteria

1. All sides indicated
   (One of the most obtuse angles may be rounded.)

 not:

2. No evidence of directional confusion at the corners   not:

3. Overlap clearly shown, but not extreme   not:

Score 1

No Score

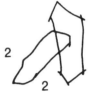

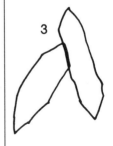

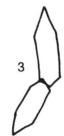

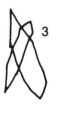

70

Supplemental Information

Age	Developmental Trends	Random Samples at Each Age
4-0	Single, outline forms	
4-4	One or two closed forms	
6-0	Touching or overlapping	
6-6		
7-6		
8-6		
10-2	Acceptable	
12-0	Fairly clean and accurate	

General spatial organization of the forms is achieved about age 6-0, with gradual improvement in the coordination of parts until age 10-2, when all parts are roughly organized. The points of form intersection are not always accurate, however. True command of the form as a coordinated whole is not achieved consistently until age 12 or 13.

On this and other complex forms, older children sometimes sketch and/or plot with dots. These behaviors are acceptable if they are not used to correct errors.

Distortions made by older children tend to be rather obvious. One of the most frequent is separation of the two figures.

FORM 23 Horizontal Diamond  Age Norm:10-11

Scoring Criteria

1. Four good corners (openings under 1/16")   not:

2. Both acute angles 60° or less   not:

3. Horizontal axis within 170°-190°   not:

4. Shortest side at least 2/3 of longest side   not:

Score 1	**No Score**

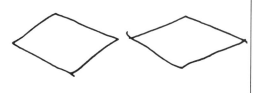

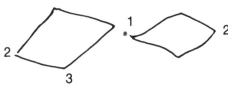

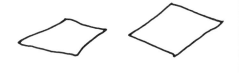

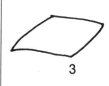

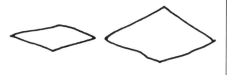

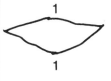

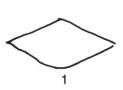

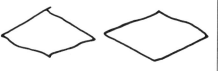

Supplemental Information

Trend Summary	

Age	Developmental Trends	Random Samples at Each Age
4-0	Closed, angular form	
4-4	Flat square or rectangle	
5-4	Attempts at rotation	
6-0	Rotated square	
6-6	Definite elongation	
8-0		
9-0		
10-11	Balance and correct angularity	

Gesell (63) indicated that 9% of 5-year-olds and 61% of 6-year-olds reproduced this horizontal diamond adequately. The lateral angles (45°) of Form 20 are more acute than those of the Gesell diamond, which accounts for a large part of the discrepancy in age norms between the two.

The tendency to reproduce a squared form is even stronger in the horizontal diamond than it is in the vertical diamond. This empirical finding perhaps has to do with the vertical-horizontal illusion.

The criteria and the score/no score examples are similar for both the vertical and the horizontal diamonds. However, the horizontal diamond is scored less strictly.

FORM 24 Three-Dimensional Rings

Scoring Criteria

1. Three complete, double-line circles   not:

2. All circles overlap   not:

3. At least one clean 3-D overlap   not:

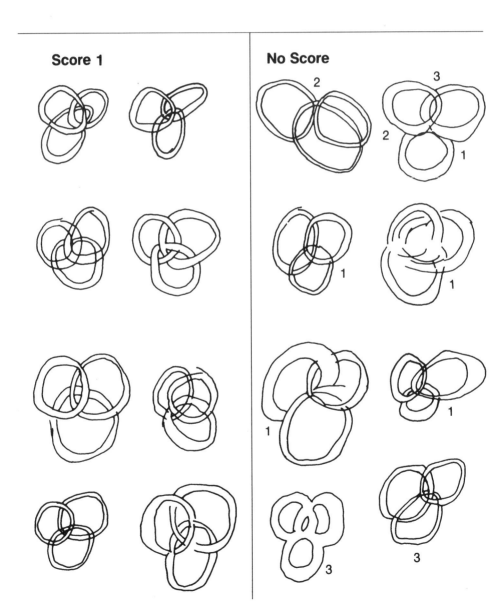

Score 1   No Score

Supplemental Information

Trend Summary	

Age	Developmental Trends	Random Samples at Each Age
4-3	Various circle groupings	
5-6	Fair grouping; single-line circles	
6-8	Double circles and better positioning	
11-2	One or more three-dimensional overlappings	See examples on preceding page.

The first successful attempts usually result after the child has constructed one complete double-lined circle with the second and third circles touching the edges of the first.

FORM 25 Necker Cube

Scoring Criteria

1. Correct number of parts   not:

2. Correct orientation   not:

3. No evidence of confusion   not:

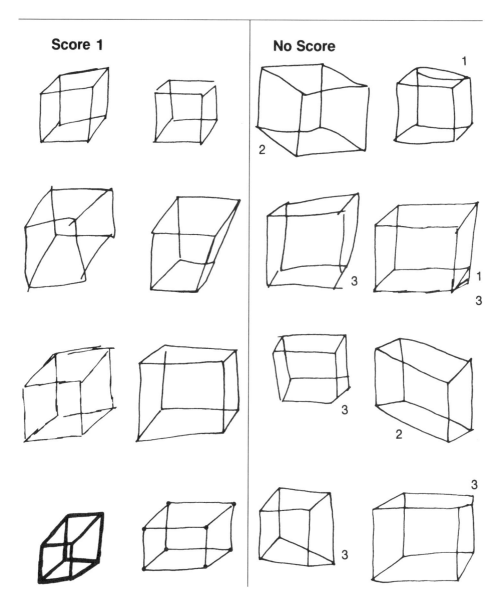

Score 1   **No Score**

Supplemental Information

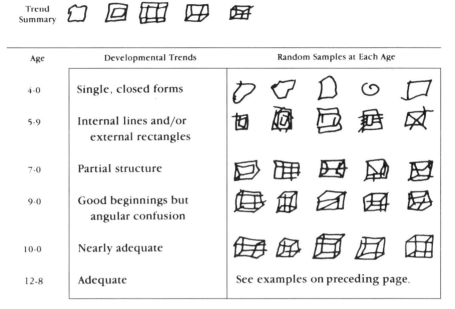

Age	Developmental Trends	Random Samples at Each Age
4-0	Single, closed forms	
5-9	Internal lines and/or external rectangles	
7-0	Partial structure	
9-0	Good beginnings but angular confusion	
10-0	Nearly adequate	
12-8	Adequate	See examples on preceding page.

In the reproductions of this form, it is common to find all aspects of the figure reversed, rather than portions. That is, part-whole perception is preserved, but directionality seems to be ignored. When a child does not perceive the reversed copy as different from the model, this indicates oversight of directionality. The child who truly saw things backward would also see the copy backward and would notice that it was different from the model.

Reproduction of this form may depend more upon cognitive analysis than is the case with other forms in the sequence. Perceiving the cube as two squares that overlap at one corner and are joined at corresponding corners by diagonals seems to facilitate its reproduction.

FORM 26 Tapered Box

Age Norm: 13-2

Scoring Criteria

1. Outer form a parallelogram (may be square) not:

2. Inner form a horizontal rectangle not:

3. Inner form clearly shifted right and down not:
   (Lower-right diagonal line the shortest)

4. No confusion or distortion not:

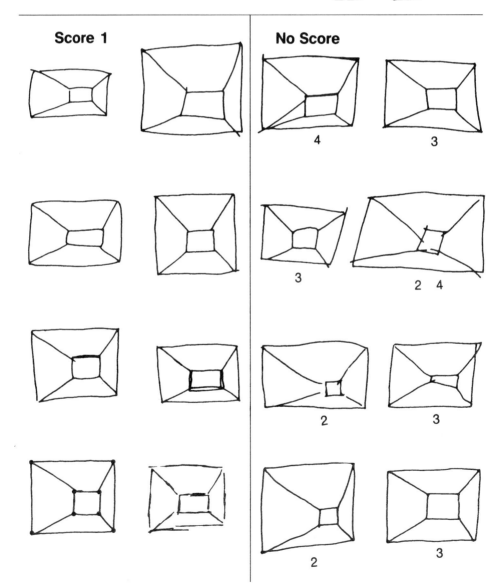

Supplemental Information

Age	Developmental Trends	Random Samples at Each Age
3-0	Scribbling	
4-0	Circles or squares	
5-0	Inner lines	
5-7	Diagonal lines	
5-11	All parts shown; tends to be squared and symmetrical	
7-0	Somewhat neater; some rectangularity	
8-6	Outer form rectangular; inner form shifts right	
9-0	Inner form rectangular	
10-0	Little change	
11-0	Neater, especially at intersections	
13-2	Inner form shifts downward.	
14-6	Almost total integration of proportion and space	

The general trend of development is not always additive. A relatively early achievement such as rectangularity of the outer form may disappear temporarily during the achievement of a later feature, such as shifting downward of the inner form. When correct position of the inner form is first attempted, the outer form again tends to become square. There is a strong tendency to exaggerate a new achievement; for example, the inner form is often shifted much more than is necessary.

79

FORM 27 Three-Dimensional Star

Scoring Criteria

1. All corners of triangles extend beyond opposing sides

2. One over- and one underlapping of the same triangle

3. No extreme distortion

not: ⋈

Score 1	**No Score**

Supplemental Information

Age	Developmental Trends	Random Samples at Each Age
4-6	Closed, angular form	
5-6	Two single-line triangles	
8-0	Double-line triangles	
11-0	Three-dimensional, but inadequate	
13-8	Adequate	See examples on preceding page.

Particular care should be exercised in determining whether both overlapping and underlapping have been achieved on the same triangle. It is common, but unacceptable, for part or all of one triangle to be superimposed upon the second.

Summary Scoring

No.	Form	Criteria	Score	No Score
1 & 4		Over ½ of lines within 30° vertical		
2 & 5		Over ½ of lines within 30° horizontal		
3 & 6		Height/width no more than 2 to 1		
7		1. Two intersecting lines 2. All parts at least ¼″ 3. At least ½ line within 20°		
8		1. Single line (extensions OK) 2. ½+ within 110°–160° 3. No abrupt change of direction		
9		Four clearly defined sides		
10		1. Single line (extensions OK) 2. ½+ within 20°–70° 3. No abrupt change of direction		
11		1. Two intersecting lines 2. Angles 20°–70° and 110°–160° 3. Long part no more than twice short		
12		1. Three clearly defined sides 2. One corner higher than others		
13		1. <¹⁄₁₆″ gap/lap 3. 2 to 1 heights 2. No distortions 4. Bisector OK		
14		1. All intersect 3. <15° 2. <⅛″ gap horizontal 4. <10° diagonals		
15		1. Not reversed 3. No misdirection 2. Sharp points 4. Long <2 × short		

No.	Form	Criteria	Score	No Score
Summary Scoring				
16		1. Seven openings 2. One circle clearly below others		
17		1. Six circles 2. Base + sides straight 3. <10° horizontal 4. <2 to 1 spacing same side		
18		1. Four corners 2. < 10° axes 3. Closed corner 4. ¹⁄₁₆″ gap/lap 5. ⅓ contact 6. < 2 to 1 heights		
19		1. Good corners 2. 170°–190° 3. No dogears 4. >⅔ sides 5. <60° angles		
20		1. Two triangles 2. 2 touch ⅓ (3rd ¹⁄₁₆″) 3. 60°–120° left 4. 100°+ slope		
21		1. Eight dots, circles, or dashes 2. No 3 centers on straight line 3. <2 to 1 longest/shortest space		
22		1. All sides (one obtuse curve OK) 2. No confusion at corners 3. Overlap not extreme		
23		1. Good corners 2. 170°–190° 3. sides >⅔ 4. 60° angles		
24		1. 3 complete, double-lined circles 2. All circles overlap 3. At least one clean 3-D overlap		
25		1. Correct number of parts 2. Correct orientation 3. No confusion		
26		1. Outer parallelogram 2. Inner rectangle 3. Right and down 4. No confusion		
27		1. All corners extended beyond sides 2. Over and underlapping, same △ 3. No extreme distortion		

Supplemental Tests

Supplemental, standardized *Visual Perception* and *Motor Coordination* tests are now provided as a means for statistically assessing visual and motor contributions to *VMI* performance. Please see page 21-22 for more information regarding the relationships between the *VMI* and the supplemental tests.

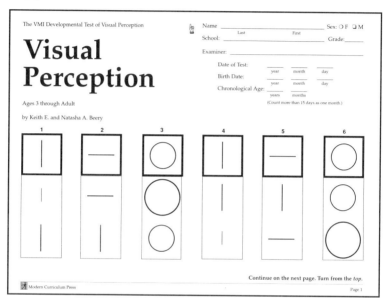

Visual Perception Administration

1. *Visual Perception* is a supplemental, standardized test that should be administered individually *after*, not before, the *VMI*.

2. Young children usually are able to proceed directly, without a rest, from the *VMI* to the *Visual*.

3. Be prepared with a stopwatch or timepiece that provides seconds. Exactly 3 minutes are allowed for this test.

4. Be sure children under 6 years of age do not have a pencil or pen available for this test. A young child's fingers need a rest after copying. Also, if they are allowed to mark, young children tend to mark every possible response on tests of this kind!

5. Do not cover parts of the form to reduce visual distractions, as that can invalidate the norms.

6. Place one finger on the heavy black outline of stimulus box 1 and keep it there until it is time for item 2.

7. Say: *See this line? There is one more line which is just the same down below.* Sweep one finger of your other hand downward from the stimulus box to the response area and say: *Let's find it! You point to it!*

8. If the child responds, you make a small mark next to the choice, whether the choice is correct or not. If the child does not respond, mark the item number above the stimulus box, as shown for item #1 below.

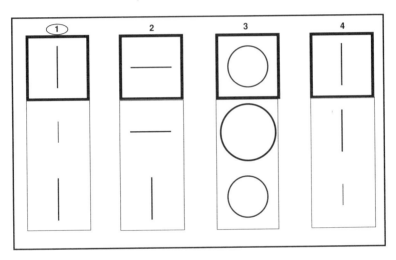

9. Whether the child responds or not, and whether the choice is correct or not, *teach* the task. Point to the too-small vertical line just below stimulus box 1. Say: *It's not this one, is it? This line is smaller* than the one in the box up above.

10. Point to the second response option, the correctly-sized vertical line below the too-small vertical line. Say: *It's this one, isn't it? It's just the same as* the one in the box up above.

11. Point to stimulus box 2, the first horizontal line, and say: *Point to the other line down below that is the same as this one.* Then continue with the same test-and-teach procedure used for item 1.

12. Point to the stimulus box 3, the first circle, and say. *Point to the other circle down below that is the same as this one.* Then continue with the same test-and-teach procedure used for items 1 and 2.

13. Starting with item 4, do not teach further.

14. Start your stopwatch and/or mark down your starting time in minutes and seconds.

15. As needed, start every item, from item 4 on, by pointing to the stimulus box and saying: *Point to the other one that is just the same as this one.* (Otherwise some children forget the concept.)

16. Continue to mark all of a young child's responses, whether correct or incorrect. You can allow children over 6 years of age to mark their own responses if you know they will handle the task appropriately. Have them make a small mark next to their choices, as shown on the preceding page. Have them draw an X through any choice they first choose, then reject.

17. Observe and record any evidence of visual acuity problems, such as squinting, positioning the head close to the paper, eye rubbing, or comments.

18. Conclude testing exactly 3 minutes and 0 seconds after starting item 4.

19. Say: *Good job! You really tried on even the ones that are hard for older boys and girls!*

20. If you have doubts about the child's visual acuity, refer the child to the school nurse or otherwise obtain a visual acuity assessment.

Visual Scoring

1. Correct responses are checked in the illustrations on the following page.

2. Starting with item 1, score the child's *first* response to each item, *before* teaching it.

3. Score only the *first* response if more than one response is given to an item, unless the child *clearly self*-corrects a choice, such as by verbalizing, "*No, not that one; this one.*"

4. As with the *VMI*, just 1 point is awarded for each correct item up to 3 consecutive incorrect items or the 3 minute time limit, whichever comes first. Including the initial 3 testing-teaching items, a maximum of 27 points can be earned.

Figure 1
Visual Perception Scoring Key

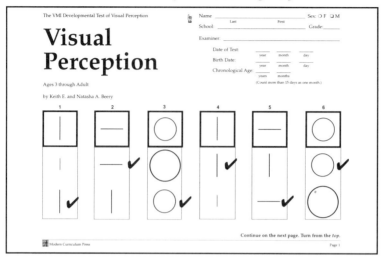

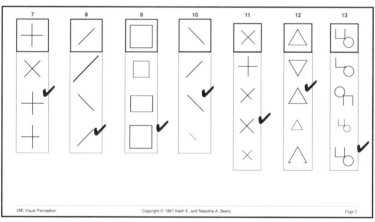

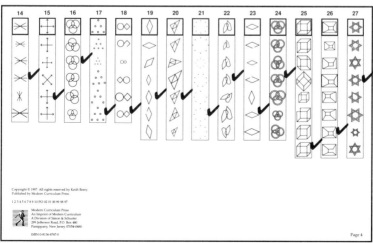

Motor Coordination Administration

1. *Motor Coordination* is a supplemental, standardized test which should be administered individually *after,* not before, the *VMI* and the *Visual Perception* tests.

2. Decide if rest and/or exercise is needed before proceeding with children below 7 years of age. From 2nd grade on, children typically have no problem in doing all three standardized tests (*VMI, Visual,* and *Motor*) without a rest.

3. Be prepared with a stopwatch or timepiece that provides seconds. Exactly 5 minutes are allowed for this test.

4. As with the *VMI,* us*e a soft, sharpened pencil or a ballpoint pen. Do not allow erasures!*

5. Keep the paper straight and centered, as in the *VMI.*

6. Say: *Watch me draw a clear, dark line from the black dot to the gray dot and try to stay inside the road.* Then, *you* draw such a line inside the item 1A road as an example.

7. Point to the 1B road and say: *Now you do it. Draw a clear, dark line from the black dot to the gray dot. Try to stay inside the road.*

8. If the child does not respond, record non-response by circling or otherwise marking the 1B item number. Then trace over your line on item 1A and repeat your instruction for item 1B.

9. If the child still does not respond, hold the child's hand and guide it to make the line in item 1B. Repeat as needed.

10. Continue to test/teach as needed to complete items 2B and 3B, using the same procedures as for item 1B.

11. Starting with item 4, with the exceptions noted in instruction 14 below, do not teach other than to say, for so long as necessary: *Draw a clear, dark line from the black dots to the gray dots. Try to stay inside the road.*

12. Start your stopwatch and/or mark down your starting time in minutes and seconds.

13. Say: *Go ahead. Do as many as you can. But do not rush. Draw carefully. Draw the forms in order. Do not skip any.*

14. You can briefly coach, if necessary, as follows:

- If a child completes a form, such as item 7, without lifting the pencil, you can say, after the child is finished: *Go ahead and lift your pencil to start new lines, like this.* Demonstrate how to draw that form on blank space *outside* the "roads."

- For items 14 through 18 *only:* if a child omits a part, such as an arrow tip on item 15, coach *one time per item* by pointing to the small stimulus above the "roads" and saying: *Have you done all the parts you see in the little one? Be sure to do all of the parts on yours!*

15. When the child has completed the first page, turn to the next page and continue by saying: *Some forms on this page have only a few dots and some do not have any dots at all. If a form has a black dot, start there. If it has no dot, start wherever you like. Stay within the roads and make each form look like the small example just above it.*

16. Do *not* stop after the child has made 3 consecutive errors. Continue for exactly 5 minutes unless a child is becoming too tired or is clearly unable to score more points. If you stop before a full 5 minutes is up, record exactly how minutes and seconds it was when you stopped.

17. Children often want to do more. If you allow a child to continue beyond the 5-minute time limit for scoring, note the last form done *within* the 5-minute time limit on the *VMI SUMMARY* chart.

Motor Scoring

1. The purpose of the *Motor* test is to assess a child's ability to control finger and hand movements. The task here is to see if the child can draw within a targeted area. Thus, the child needs only to draw within all the "roads." Motor drawings do *not* have to meet the *VMI* criteria shown on pages 34-81.

2. Score *all* of the forms attempted within 5 minutes. Do *not* stop scoring after 3 consecutive failures!

3. An item is scored 1 point if the response meets *all three* (a, b, and c) of the following criteria:

   a. There are pencil marks within *all* parts of the roads and between all dots.

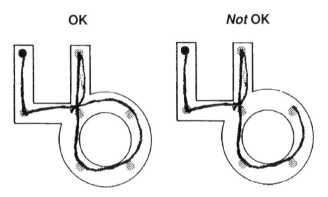

     • The marks do *not* have to be *complete.*

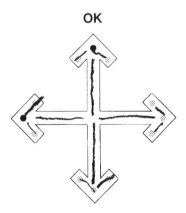

b. No mark *clearly* goes *over* a road line. But, it is OK to touch or even be *on* a road line, and space need not show between the line and outside road.

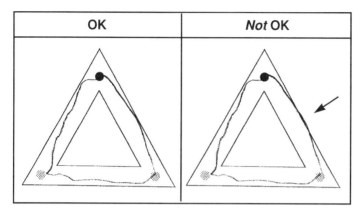

- Exception: If a line *touches* a dot and goes too far out the *square* end of a road, that is OK.

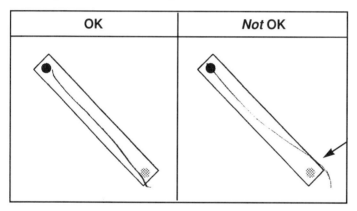

c. Three dimensional (3-D) overlaps on Forms #24 and #27 must be shown.

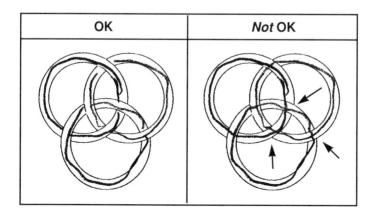

IV. Interpretation of Results

Raw and Derived Scores

Raw scores are of little use by themselves. However, raw scores can be converted to a number of derived, or normalized, scores that enable comparisons of one individual's performance to those of a normative population. Derived scores also allow meaningful comparisons to be made between different tests and between the same test administered at different times. It is important to realize, however, that derived scores from some tests are more valid than derived scores from other tests, depending upon each test's basic reliability and validity. Besides the major types of derived scores described below, others exist, such as T-scores and z-scores. Consult a current tests and measurement text for further information about other scales in which you may be interested.

Major Sources of Derived Score Error

Normative Population Ideally, every test would be *locally* normed on every population for which it will be used. Since such extensive local norming is not practical, the next best norming population is one that is as representative as possible of the state or national population in which it will be used. Locally normed tests should not be used nationally. Test selectors should always compare the average performance levels of even nationally normed tests with those of other well-established and nationally normed tests. Consult good test review texts (34,157,158).

Standard Error of Measurement (SEM) All types of derived scores contain some degree of statistical imprecision simply because they are based upon mathematical probabilities. However, the degree of measurement error can vary widely from test to test, depending upon how reliable each is. The standard error of measurement (SEM) of each test varies and is an important tool for estimating a *range* of scores within which an obtained score might actually fall. Add and subtract 1 SEM from an obtained score to find the range within which the true score should fall about two-thirds of the time. Add and subtract 2 SEMs to find the range within which the true score should fall 95 percent of the time. An example is given on page 94.

Standard Scores

Standard scores are equal units of measurement with a mean of 100 and a standard deviation of 15. Thus, the difference in performance between standard scores of 100 and 110 is the same as the difference in performance between standard scores of 150 and 160. Therefore, standard scores can be added together, averaged, and otherwise treated mathematically, which is a great advantage for research and other purposes. Because IQ scores are standard scores and have become familiar to many people, the relative levels of performance represented by standard scores are often easy to communicate.

Table 1
Standard Score Interpretation

Standard Score	Performance	% of Age Group
133-160	Very High	2
118-132	High	14
83-117	Average	68
68-82	Low	14
40-67	Very Low	2

How are standard scores and standard errors of measurement (SEMs) related? Using the *VMI* as an example, if an obtained standard score on the *VMI* is 100, the statistically *true* score may actually be somewhere between 95 and 105 for most age groups, as the SEM for a *VMI* standard score is about plus or minus 5 points. See pages 96 and 107-108 for more about *VMI* SEMs.

One of the beauties of standard scores is that they enable valid statistical comparisons between different tests, including test results from the current *VMI* with any of its previous scoring systems.

Scaled Scores

Scaled scores have the same basic statistical properties as standard scores except that they have a mean of 10 and a standard deviation of 3, which makes them rougher (more general) measurements than standard scores. Scaled and standard scores can easily be converted with one another by means of a table such as Table 15 on page 176. In spite of their parallel relationship, most parents and others do not as easily understand differences in scaled scores as they do standard scores.

Stanines, NCE's, and Other Normalized Scores

These scores, like scaled scores, are essentially the same as standard scores, but have different means and standard deviations. Each has its advantages and disadvantages for research and other practical purposes. Stanines, for example, have a mean of 5 and a standard deviation of 2. This makes stanines even rougher (more general) measurements than scaled scores.

Percentiles

Although percentiles also have a parallel relationship with standard scores and other normalized scores, they differ significantly. Percentiles are not equal units of measurement. That is, the difference between the 50th and the 60th percentiles is much smaller than the difference between the 70th and the 80th percentiles. Thus, percentiles cannot legitimately be added, averaged, or otherwise treated mathematically like standard scores. Even so, percentiles are useful for communication purposes with many people because they are familiar.

Age and Grade Equivalents

Once more it should be stressed that although age and grade equivalents are still in popular use, they should be used with caution, if at all, according to leading test experts and professional organizations (1). Because they are not equal units of measurement, they are easily misinterpreted. Age equivalent information is provided on page 144 because some institutions still require these scores.

Profiles

The Profile box on the *VMI* test booklet cover, shown on page 96, provides a convenient place to record and chart standard scores, percentiles, and other *VMI* raw score equivalents. Test results for the *Visual Perception* and *Motor Coordination* supplemental tests also can be recorded here. If you wish to graphically show a student's relative strengths and weaknesses, perhaps for purposes of communication with the student or parents, this profile can be useful. The booklet cover facilitates easy filing and quick research reference, as it contains the child's name and birth date.

An individual strength, in comparison to the *normative* population, is indicated by a test score which is above *average*, and a weakness is indicated by a test score which is below *average*. Schools often define *average* as the middle 50 percent of scores between the 25th and 75 percentiles. Another common definition of *average* is one standard deviation below and above the mean, the middle 68 percent of the normative population. If this latter definition is used, standard scores between 85 and 115 are average for each of the *VMI* tests. Standard score equivalents for raw scores, according to children's chronological ages, are provided on pages 146-175.

The Beery-Buktenica
Developmental Test of Visual-Motor Integration

VMI

Ages 3 through Adult (FULL FORMAT)

by Keith E. Beery and Norman A. Buktenica

Name _____ Sex: ○ F ❑ M
                Last   First
School: _____ Grade:_____

Examiner: _____

Date of Test: _____
                year   month   day
Birth Date: _____
                year   month   day
Chronological Age: _____
                years   months
(Count more than 15 days as one month.)

SUMMARY				PROFILE				
See the VMI 1997 Manual for norms.			Standard	VMI	Visual	Motor	Percentile
	VMI	Visual	Motor	145	-	-	-	99.7
				140	-	-	-	99.2
Raw Scores:	____	____	____	135	-	-	-	99
				130	-	-	-	98
Standard Scores:	____	____	____	125	-	-	-	95
				120	-	-	-	91
Scaled Scores:	____	____	____	115	-	-	-	84
				110	-	-	-	75
Percentiles:	____	____	____	105	-	-	-	63
				100	-	-	-	50
Other Scaling:	____	____	____	95	-	-	-	37
				90	-	-	-	25
Comments and Recommendations				85	-	-	-	16
				80	-	-	-	9
				75	-	-	-	5
				70	-	-	-	2
				65	-	-	-	1
				60	-	-	-	.8
				55	-	-	-	.3

Begin testing at the back. Turn booklet over with bound edge toward the student. If subtests are used, always test in this order: VMI → Visual → Motor.

Modern Curriculum Press

Remember, no test is exact. The *true* score of an individual may fall within a range of scores that is dependent upon the standard error of measurement (SEM) of that particular test. Therefore, if you want to compare an individual's *VMI* test score to another *score*, such as a score from the *VMI's* supplemental *Visual* or *Motor* tests, each of the tests' SEMs should be taken into consideration. For example, if a child receives standard scores of 90 on the *VMI* and 100 on *Visual*, the two scores are probably not significantly different, as their SEMs overlap. If 1 SEM is added and subtracted from each score, the true *VMI* score would be between 85 and 95 and the true *Visual* score would be between 94 and 106. The two bands overlap between 94 and 95, so one cannot be confident that the true scores are statistically different. More information about SEMs and other measurement interpretation basics are provided on pages 107-108.

Some test batteries provide a composite score, which is essentially an average of all the subtests that have been administered. A composite score is not provided for the *VMI*, because it is believed that such scores are often meaningless, as they attempt to average together very different processes or skills.

Comparability of Scores

The 4-point scores of the 1989 *VMI* scoring system correlated almost perfectly (.98) with earlier 1-point scoring (9). And, as mentioned earlier, such scores can be validly compared, because standard scores enable comparison of scores even between very different tests.

The same standard score and other derived score tables apply for both the short, 18-item and the full, 27-item booklet versions of the VMI. However, for valid results, the 18-item version should not be used with children older than 8 years and 0 months of age.

Pryzwansky and others (38,144) have reported that there has been no significant difference in results for *VMI* group and individual administrations.

V. Normative Procedures

Item and Format Selection

VMI On the basis of an extensive review of literature and clinical experience, 72 geometric forms were initially selected for study (8). Geometric forms were selected over alphabetic, numeric, or other forms in an effort to minimize cultural and educational influences. About 600 children between the ages of 2 and 15 years copied the 72 forms with paper and pencil in various formats, similar to the current *VMI* format. Item analyses were made of the results, new forms were constructed, old forms were modified, and a developmental sequence of 30 forms was created. The criteria for selection were: (1) A form had to fit into the chronological age scale at a point where there was no form established for that age, (2) the chronological age at which reproduction of a form occurred had to be relatively clear-cut, (3) the chronological age at which substages of reproduction of a form occurred had to be clear-cut, and (4) there could not be a wide difference in the chronological ages at which boys and girls reproduced a form.

These 30 forms were administered to another 600 children. Following an item analysis of results from the 30-item sequence, 24 forms were selected for the final sequence. The criteria for selection of the final 24 items were the same as the those used earlier, but included two additional requirements: (1) The sequence had to include relatively more forms appropriate for the preschool and kindergarten age range in order to enhance its usefulness for early identification screening, and (2) the developmental age norms of individual forms, identified by the results of current and previous samples, had to be within four months of each other. In essence, this was a cross-validation procedure. Items that were not stable from sample to sample were eliminated.

Evidence that item selection was successful is presented in the Rasch-Wright item analysis and other indices reported on pages 105 to 107, as well as the developmental growth curve presented on page 114.

A variety of format variables were studied, including the size and placement of stimulus forms on papers of various sizes, orientations, thickness, and colors. White paper tended to cause glare and allowed stimulus and response lines to show through the paper, thereby causing both distraction and other uncontrolled variables. Test booklets that opened in the usual front-to-back manner were seriously flawed because pencil impressions both showed through and created bumps in the response areas on the following page. The orientation of the paper also proved to be important. Since many forms are more difficult to reproduce in certain orientations, children often rotated vertically oriented pages in order to simplify their tasks.

Such rotation and other location problems were addressed by printing the stimuli at the *top* of *horizontally* oriented 11″ by 8.5″ pages. Glare and translucency were corrected by using *green* paper. Pencil impressions on unused sheets were eliminated by simply reversing the order of the sheets, so that the child started at the *back,* or last, page and worked forward.

Supplemental Tests Item selection for the *Visual Perception* and *Motor Coordination* supplemental tests was straight-forward. The *same* geometric forms used in the *VMI* are used in the supplemental tests, which makes comparisons between performances on all three tests as valid as possible. Other test batteries attempting to emulate the *VMI* have used geometric forms for their form-copying tests, but have used quite different stimuli and/or tasks for their visual and motor subtests, which contaminates test comparisons.

For practical reasons, the size of the geometric forms on both supplemental tests had to vary from the *VMI*. For example, if the same sized forms were used on the *Visual* test, a *very* lengthy booklet for it would be required. Although the *Visual* forms are considerably smaller than those on the *VMI*, experimentation has demonstrated that even very small children effectively deal with them unless a significant visual acuity problem is present. As in any visual-motor evaluation, examiners should be alert for and assess possible visual problems.

The sizes of the stimulus forms on the *Motor* supplemental test are comparable to those on the *VMI*. However, it is not possible, or at least practical, to construct a *pure* supple-mental motor coordination test for a test like the *VMI*. A visual component to such a task has to be present. The practical goal is to make the visual component as easy as possible. Therefore, visual examples of forms, dots, and path guides are provided in the *Motor* supplemental test.

Sample Selection and Demographics

The *VMI* was originally normed in 1964 on 1,030 Illinois children. It was cross-validated in 1981 with 2,060 California children and again in 1989 with a national sample of 2,734 children. It also has been normed in other countries. The *VMI* norms over time and place have been consistent, particularly at the preschool and elementary grades levels for which it was designed.

The *VMI* and its supplemental *Visual* and *Motor* tests were normed in 1996 on 2,614 children from 3 to 18 years of age, from the 5 major sections of the United States. School psychologists and learning disabilities specialists from all 50 states were randomly selected from professional organization listings. These specialists were asked by mail to respond to a survey regarding their school population compositions and of their personal willingness to serve as norming supervisors and/or examiners. Samples were selected, in an effort to adequately reflect the 1990 U.S. census, from classes with representative ranges of learning abilities in California, Connecticut, New Mexico, New York, North Dakota, Mississippi, Missouri, Oklahoma, South Carolina, and Washington. A total of 26 childcare, preschool, public, and private schools participated.

As shown in Tables 2 and 3, the 1996 norming samples were collectively representative of the 1990 U.S. census. The socioeconomic levels of the samples were estimated by the norming supervisors on the basis of their local aid for dependent children (AFDC) and other available data. According to the 1990 national census, the bottom 21 percent of households in the United States of America earned under $15,000 in 1989, and the top 21 percent earned over $50,000 (180).

Norming test data were collected between November, 1995, and January, 1996. All of the children in the sample classes, including those with disabling conditions, were included in the norming data. All of the children were administered the *VMI*, *Visual*, and *Motor* tests, in that order. All scoring of the protocols was done by the author and his research assistants.

Table 2
Demographic Characteristics of the Normative Sample

Characteristics	Sample Percentage	U.S. Census Percentage
Gender		
Female	49	49
Male	51	51
Ethnicity		
African-American	14	14
Hispanic	12	11
Native American	1	1
Oriental-Pacific Island	3	3
Other	70	71
Residence		
Rural	11	9
Suburban	68	69
Urban	21	22
Geographic Area		
East	21	20
North Central	24	24
South	32	35
West	23	21
Socioeconomic		
High (>$50,000/year)	19	21
Middle	56	58
Low (<$15,000/year)	23	21

Age	Number		
3	204	8	
4	221	8	
5	219	8	
6	227	9	
7	212	8	
8	195	7	
9	216	8	
10	202	8	
11	179	7	
12	132	5	
13	131	5	
14	133	5	
15	134	5	
16	106	4	
17	103	4	
Total	2614	100	

Age:	3	4	5	6	7	8	9	10	11	12	13	14	15	16	17
Gender															
Female	48	51	47	49	53	46	48	48	53	45	49	47	53	46	49
Male	52	49	53	51	47	54	52	52	47	55	51	53	47	54	51
Ethnicity															
African-American	15	13	15	14	15	10	12	16	13	10	14	15	15	16	15
Hispanic	11	13	12	12	11	13	11	10	11	14	11	11	12	10	13
Native American	1	2	1	1	1	2	2	1	1	3	1	1	1	2	1
Oriental-Pacific Is.	2	4	3	1	2	2	3	4	3	5	2	3	7	1	2
Other	71	68	69	72	71	73	72	69	72	68	72	70	65	71	69
Socioeconomic															
High	16	18	18	20	17	19	19	20	18	17	17	19	24	22	23
Middle	58	58	59	58	59	59	58	57	61	61	59	60	56	55	56
Low	26	24	23	22	24	22	23	23	21	22	24	21	20	23	21
Geographic															
East	22	21	23	22	22	20	19	21	21	18	23	22	19	20	21
North Central	25	24	24	26	25	23	24	23	21	25	22	23	23	25	24
South	35	34	32	32	33	35	34	34	33	32	31	30	29	28	30
West	18	21	21	20	20	22	23	22	25	25	24	25	29	27	25

Standard Scores

Cumulative frequency distributions of raw scores were created for each age group between ages 3-0 and 18-0. Normalized developmental curves were drawn from these distributions and were smoothed slightly, based on frequency distributions at 3-month age intervals. Normalized standard scores were then read and interpolated from the distributions. The resulting standard score equivalents for raw scores will be found in Table 14 on pages 146-175.

Other Derived Scores

Percentile equivalents for standard scores which are available in basic statistical textbooks are presented in Table 15 on page 176. Other scaled equivalents of standard scores will be found in that table. Age equivalents for raw scores were read from the normalized developmental curves shown on pages 114-115, and are presented in Table 13 on page 145.

See Chapter IV regarding the strengths and limitations of age equivalent and other scores. Age equivalent scores are presented because some institutions still require them, but they should be used with caution.

VI. Reliability

Tests must measure with a high degree of consistency if they are to be valid and, therefore, useful. The reliability of tests such as the *VMI* requires that there be adequate consistency in: (1) the content of its items, (2) individuals' performances on the test when it is readministered, and (3) scoring performed by different examiners. The overall reliability of a test should be at least .70 for research purposes, .80 or higher for screening tests such as the *VMI*, and .90 or more for making more important decisions about an individual (76,157,158).

Content Sampling

As reported earlier, items for the *VMI* were selected after a review of literature, and extensive experimental and empirical research (8). Rasch-Wright analysis assesses how well the test items selected consistently follow the direction of the author's test construct, how well the items are separated from one another, and how well they differentiate among individuals (198). The Rasch-Wright results for a random sample of 50 individuals from each age group of the norming data are shown in Table 4, page 106.

Rasch-Wright and other measures of internal consistency are most appropriate for *power* tests, those in which the test taker is not pressured in some way to work speedily. Rasch-Wright and other such measures are not applicable for *highly speeded* tests. The reliability of such tests needs to be measured by test-retest and other statistics. The *VMI*'s two supplemental tests are timed. Thus, although almost all children either finish these tests or have ceased to make correct responses within the time limits, both supplemental tests are technically only *quasi*-power tests. Taken in this perspective, the Rasch-Wright results for the supplemental tests are provided for informational purposes. Because the sample sizes and range of scores of the age groups are necessarily restricted, their coefficients are smaller than for the total sample, as would be expected. The Rasch-Wright results indicate high content reliability for the *VMI*, as its total group item separation was 1.00 and its total group person separation was .96.

Internal Consistency How homogeneous are the test items? A traditional statistical method for answering that question is to assess how well children perform on half of the 24 directly-copied forms compared with the other half

Table 4
Rasch-Wright Item Separations by Age and Total Sample
(Decimals Omitted)

Age	VMI		Visual		Motor	
	Item	Person	Item	Person	Item	Person
3	98	95	96	91	96	90
4	99	94	96	89	97	89
5	98	89	97	90	96	89
6	97	87	96	89	95	86
7	96	84	97	84	91	85
8	98	85	95	83	92	85
9	96	80	96	83	93	89
10	97	80	95	84	92	85
11	96	82	94	85	94	85
12	96	86	92	81	91	86
13	96	84	93	79	90	81
14	94	80	91	78	89	84
15	95	76	91	77	93	79
16	95	75	93	76	91	76
17	96	83	92	81	90	77
Means:	96	84	94	83	93	84
Totals:	100	96	100	93	100	93

of the forms. The Spearman-Brown corrected results of correlating the odd and even items for the same 750 children in the Rasch-Wright analyses are shown in Table 5, page 107. Again, as they are merely *quasi*-power tests, internal consistency results for the *VMI*'s *Visual* and *Motor* supplemental tests are provided for informational purposes. Because their sample sizes and range of scores are necessarily restricted, age group coefficients are smaller than those for the total sample. Table 5 indicates that the *VMI* had an 1996 overall odd-even split-half correlation of .88. In the 1988 *VMI* norming studies, odd-even correlations ranged from .76 to .91, with a median value of .85. Other studies of full ability ranges of kindergarten through high school students prior to 1996 have yielded single-grade split-half correlations ranging from .53 to .92, with a median of .78 (9,23,29,61,112,155).

Coefficient alpha is another traditional means for measuring internal consistency. In effect, it splits and correlates items in every possible way and yields the same results as Kuder-Richardson formula 20. Alpha coefficients are typically lower than other internal consistency coefficients. Using the 24 direct-copy items, the maximum *VMI* alpha coefficient can be only .96. The 1996 overall coefficient alpha result of .82, shown in Table 5, also provides supportive evidence for *VMI* content reliability.

Table 5
Internal Consistency by Age and Total Sample
Odd-Even (O-E) Split-Half and Coefficient Alpha

Age	VMI		Visual		Motor	
	O-E	Alpha	O-E	Alpha	O-E	Alpha
3	93	89	90	87	91	89
4	92	86	90	86	88	84
5	90	84	89	87	90	88
6	86	81	87	86	89	85
7	82	80	91	85	91	82
8	90	82	90	84	86	84
9	85	79	83	81	92	86
10	86	81	84	83	85	81
11	87	82	91	82	89	82
12	88	83	82	79	88	83
13	90	85	82	81	95	89
14	88	81	81	76	87	79
15	86	80	81	75	80	75
16	85	81	79	74	78	71
17	88	82	82	76	79	73
Means:	88	82	85	81	87	82

Standard Error of Measurement (SEM)

Statistics do not always represent reality precisely, as statistics are based upon mathematical probabilities. Typically, there is some degree of error in even the most rigorous attempts for accurate measurement.

Based upon the split-half reliability coefficients for the *VMI*, its rounded standard errors of measurement (SEMs) for standard scores (means of 100 and standard deviations of 15) are shown in Table 6. Based on the time sampling reliability coefficients for the *VMI*'s supplemental tests reported on the next page, the rounded standard score SEM for both *Visual* and *Motor* is 6. The reliability coefficients and SEMs for the *VMI* and its supplementary tests are considered more than adequate for the screening purposes for which they are intended.

Table 6
Standard Score Standard Errors of Measurement by Age
(Decimals rounded)

Age	VMI	Visual	Motor
3	4	6	6
4	4	6	6
5	5	6	6
6	6	6	6
7	6	6	6
8	5	6	6
9	6	6	6
10	6	6	6
11	5	6	6
12	5	6	6
13	5	6	6
14	5	6	6
15	6	6	6
16	6	6	6
17	5	6	6

Use and interpret these SEMs in the usual manner. For example, suppose that a 5-year-old child has a standard score of 97 on the *VMI*. If statistics were perfect, there would be no doubt that the 97 is a precise representation of how well this child performed. However, as statistics are not always precise, the student's score actually might have been somewhat higher or lower than a 97. Add and subtract the *VMI*'s SEM for 5 year olds from 97 to find the range of possible *true* scores about two-thirds of the time, a 68 percent confidence level, which is the usual confidence level applied. In our example, this child's *true* score could range from 92 to 102, as 97 minus 5 is 92 and 97 plus 5 is 102. To find the range of possible *true* scores 95 percent of the time, a 95 percent confidence level, add and subtract 2 SEMs. See page 96 for an inter-test overlap example.

Time Sampling

When the same children take the *VMI* twice, without a

special instructional program between testings, are their scores consistent? The *VMI* and its supplemental tests were administered to 122 children between the ages of 6 and 10 in regular public school classrooms which contained full ranges of student abilities and included proportionate numbers of children with disabilities. The time between the initial administration and the retest averaged 3 weeks. The overall test-retest raw score coefficients were .87 for the *VMI*, .84 for *Visual* and .83 for *Motor*.

Test-retest coefficients are commonly lower than other reliability coefficients, particularly for developmental tests over fairly long periods of time, because individual scores are expected to change with maturation or learning. Prior to 1996, reported test-retest reliabilities for the *VMI* ranged from .63 over a 7-month period with preschool children to .92 over a 2-week period with a full ability range of elementary aged children, with a median of .81 (8,93, 111,155). A correlation of .59 was obtained with institutionalized, emotionally disturbed children over a 2-week period (65).

As indicated earlier, the *VMI* has produced rather consistent norms over time and places, which includes a number of other countries. Because of this consistency (and the fact that the four-point scoring used in 1989 correlates almost perfectly, .98, with the usual *VMI* one-point scoring), *VMI* studies conducted prior to the 1996 norming can be validly reported and compared.

Interscorer Reliability

For the 1996 norming study, two individuals independently scored 100 *VMI*, *Visual*, and *Motor* tests of a random sample of the norming group. The resulting interscorer reliabilities were .94 for the *VMI*, .98 for *Visual*, and .95 for *Motor*. Prior to 1996, reported *VMI* reliability coefficients for two or more scorers have ranged from .73 to .99 for a variety of preschool through elementary aged children, with a median of .93 (8,23,66,106,132,144,155,160,168). An interscorer reliability of .99 was obtained with a sample of elementary aged children which included equal numbers of children with an average range of ability, learning disabilities, and mental retardation (160).

As part of the earlier 1981 *VMI* norming study, school psychologists taught resource teachers to administer and score the *VMI*. The resource teachers then taught classroom teachers at their schools to administer and score the tests. The formal teaching sessions varied at each school, but averaged about two hours. The on-site resource teachers were available to classroom teachers who had follow-up questions. Resulting interjudge reliabilities for a full age-range sample of 120 students were .98 between psychologists and resource teachers, .95 between resource teachers and classroom teachers, and .93 between psychologists and classroom teachers (9). Similarly, Friedman and others (56) taught inexperienced paraprofessionals to score the *VMI* and reported interscorer reliabilities exceeding .90.

However, the level of interscorer reliability, particularly for inexperienced scorers, seems to depend upon the preparation of the scorers. Pryzwansky (144) reported a correlation of .73 between scoring by a group of learning disabilities teachers and a psychology extern. This correlation was increased to .98 after a follow-up workshop. Lepkin and Pryzwansky reported interscorer reliabilities exceeding .90 between kindergarten teachers and psychology externs following 3 hours of preparation and recommended such structured workshops for scorers (106). The additional specificity added to the 1989 and 1996 *VMI* scoring criteria should, as Lepkin and Pryzwansky found, facilitate the teaching of reliable *VMI* scoring (106).

Overall Reliability

The average of Anastasi's three major reliability error sources (interscorer, internal consistency, and test-retest) provide the best indications of overall reliability (2). As shown in Table 7, the *VMI* and its supplemental *Visual* and *Motor* tests had overall average reliabilities of .92, 91, and .89 respectively.

Table 7 Summary of VMI, Visual, and Motor Reliabilities			
	VMI	Visual	Motor
Interscorer	94	98	95
Content Sampling	96	NA	NA
Time Sampling	87	84	83
Average	92	91	89

VII. Validity

In order to be considered a valid measure, a test must first be reliable, or consistent in its measurement, as discussed in the previous chapter. Additionally, a solid test must demonstrate content, concurrent, construct, and predictive validity, as well as control for bias. Each of the foregoing subjects will be addressed in this chapter.

Content Validity

Content validity is the degree to which the content of a test provides a representative sample of the behaviors the test is designed to assess. Content validity is established through the procedures used in selecting items or tasks for a test. Thus, the content validity of the *VMI* and its supplemental tests can be assessed to a great extent by the item construction and selection procedures described in Chapter V. Content validity also can be quantitatively assessed by the Rasch-Wright and other item analysis methods used for the *VMI* and its supplemental tests, as reported in Chapter VI. The content validity of the *VMI* and its supplemental tests was thereby strongly supported.

Concurrent Validity

Concurrent validity is provided by comparing the results of a test to those of other tests designed to measure similar constructs. Therefore, as a part of the 1996 norming study, the *VMI* was correlated with the Copying subtest of the *Developmental Test of Visual Perception (DTVP-2)* and the *Drawing* subtest of the *Wide Range Assessment of Visual Motor Abilities (WRAVMA)*. The tests were administered in a counterbalanced order to 122 students from regular public school classrooms, kindergarten through 5th grade. The *VMI*'s supplemental test results from these same children were correlated with those from the *DTVP-2* subtests for *Position in Space* and *Eye-Hand Coordination*. The raw score correlations are shown in Table 8 on page 112. These results generally support the validity of the *VMI* and its supplemental tests, although correlations are only moderately high between the *VMI* and the newer, less well-developed geometric form-copying tests.

Table 8 Raw Score Correlations among three VMI tests, DTVP-2, and WRAVMA (Decimals Omitted)			
	VMI	Visual	Motor
WRAVMA Drawing DTVP-2 Copying DTVP-2 Position in Space DTVP-2 Eye-Hand Coordination	52 75	62	65

With these same 122 students, for example, the *WRAVMA Drawing* test correlated .52 with the *VMI*, .44 with chronological age, and .29 with the *Comprehensive Tests of Basic Skills (CTBS)* total achievement tests. In contrast, the *VMI* correlated .80 with age and .63 with the *CTBS* total for these students.

In relation to older tests, the *VMI* has frequently been correlated with the *Bender-Gestalt*. These correlations have ranged from .29 to .93, with a moderate median of .56 (3,24,25,35,39,65,100,141,160,165,169). No significant differences in scores have been found between individual and group administration of the *VMI*, whereas *Bender* group scores have been higher than individual *Bender* scores (38,144). Also, the *VMI* is easier to use than the *Bender*, especially with inexperienced examiners (23,43,81). Breen and others (3,4,24,25,105,157,160,162,163) have found the *VMI* to be more reliable, valid, and useful than the *Bender*.

Construct Validity

Construct validity is demonstrated by identifying several constructs thought to underlie test performance, then generating hypotheses based upon those constructs and, finally, verifying the hypotheses by empirical data or logic. The following basic *VMI* constructs will be examined:

1. The abilities measured by the *VMI* and its supplemental tests are developmental. Thus, it is hypothesized that results from the tests will be related to chronological age.

2. The abilities measured by the *VMI* and its supplemental tests are related to one another because each supplemental test measures a part of the *VMI* whole. Thus, it is hypothesized that results from the tests will correlate at least moderately well with one another.

112

3. Each of the *VMI*'s supplemental tests measures a part, but not the entirety, of the *VMI* whole. Thus, it is hypothesized that there will be evidence that the *VMI* is more demanding than either of the supplemental tests alone.

4. The abilities measured by the *VMI* and its supplemental tests are related to at least non-verbal aspects of intelligence. Thus, it is hypothesized that results from the tests will correlate moderately with non-verbal intelligence test results and less well with verbal test results.

5. The abilities measured by the *VMI* and its supplemental tests are related to academic achievement. Thus, it is hypothesized that results from the tests will correlate moderately well with academic achievement test results.

6. The test items of the *VMI* and its supplemental tests measure similar respective traits and are effective in measuring persons. Thus, the Rasch-Wright item and person separation indices will be high, as shown in Table 4 on page 106.

7. The abilities measured by the *VMI* are related to certain disabling conditions. Thus, it is hypothesized that *VMI* results will be lower among such populations.

Hypothesis 1: Chronological Age The abilities measured by the *VMI* and its supplemental tests are developmental. Thus, it is hypothesized that results from the tests will be related to chronological age.

The *VMI* was specifically designed to measure changes in eye-hand coordination as children grow older. Similarly, the *VMI*'s supplemental *Visual Perception* and *Motor Coordination* tests were designed to be developmental scales. As indicated by the developmental curves shown in Figures 2 through 4 on pages 114-115, Hypothesis 1 is strongly confirmed by the 1996 norming data. The correlations for the total norming sample between chronological age and the *VMI*, *Visual*, and *Motor* were .83, .75 and . 74 respectively, all of which were significant beyond the .01 level of confidence. These findings are consistent with previous results, such as the .89 correlation between the *VMI* and chronological age in the 1989 *VMI* norming (9).

Hypothesis 2: Part-Whole Intercorrelations The abilities measured by the *VMI* and its supplemental tests are related to one another because each supplemental test measures a part of the *VMI* whole. Thus, it was hypothesized that results from the tests will correlate at least

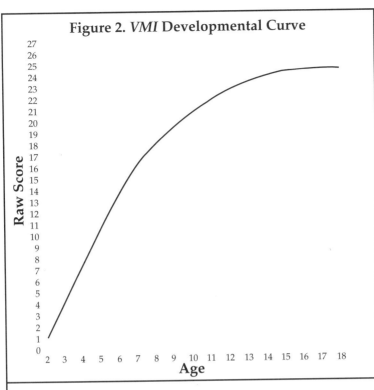

Figure 2. *VMI* Developmental Curve

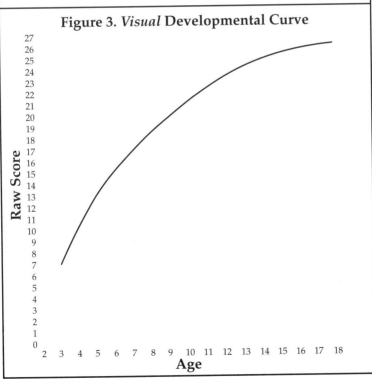

Figure 3. *Visual* Developmental Curve

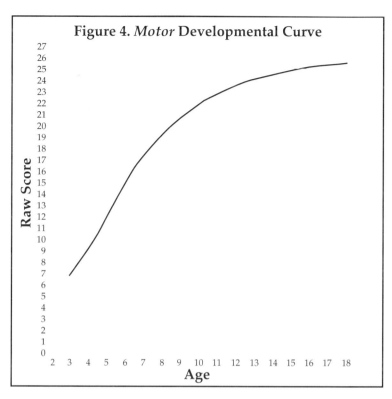

Figure 4. *Motor* Developmental Curve

Raw Score (y-axis, values 0 through 27)

Age (x-axis, values 2 through 18)

moderately well with one another. Using the entire norming sample, with all correlations significant beyond the .05 level of confidence, Table 9 on page 116 serves to confirm this hypothesis.

Hypothesis 3: Part-Whole Hierarchy Each of the *VMI's* supplemental tests measures a part, but not the entirety, of the *VMI* whole. Thus, it is hypothesized that there will be evidence the *VMI* is more demanding than either of the supplemental tests alone. On average, for the total norming population, children made one more correct response on both the *Visual* and the *Motor* tests than on the *VMI*. At early ages, children had, on average, 2 more correct responses on *Visual* and on *Motor* than they had on the *VMI*. Thus, although the supplemental (part) tests take *less* time than the *VMI* (whole) test, *more* items were completed successfully on the supplemental tests.

The foregoing finding is consistent with the original 1964 validation findings in which 164 children between the ages of 5 and 15 were able to visually discriminate 2 more and trace 4 more of the *VMI* test forms than they could copy when given all the time they wanted (8). Thus, the

Table 9
Raw Score Correlations among the VMI and its
Supplemental Visual and Motor Tests
(Decimals Omitted)

Age	VMI vs. Visual	VMI vs. Motor	Visual vs. Motor
3	31	60	31
4	41	57	43
5	53	42	44
6	42	47	15
7	35	44	40
8	24	18	46
9	27	32	53
10	34	36	48
11	31	32	25
12	35	45	39
13	42	23	43
14	36	13	40
15	36	28	17
16	22	35	20
17	27	18	24
18	58	25	27
Medians	35	33	39

VMI seems to measure an *integration* factor in addition to visual perception and motor coordination.

Even more support for this central part-whole construct is provided by other research. For example, children with spina bifida usually do relatively well on visual perceptual tests, but do poorly on the *VMI* (58,175,196). The phylogenetic and ontogenetic research reviewed on pages 16-19 is strongly supportive of this construct, as is current neurological research which posits separate *what* (visual perception) and *where* (visual-motor) neural pathways in the brain (67,152). The *VMI* whole is greater than the sum of its parts. The *VMI* does, indeed, seem to be measuring the hyphen, the *integration* aspect in the term visual-motor integration.

116

Hypothesis 4: Intelligence The abilities measured by the *VMI* and its supplemental tests are related to at least non-verbal aspects of intelligence. Thus, it is hypothesized that results from the tests will correlate moderately with non-verbal intelligence test results and less well with verbal test results. Table 10 shows correlations between the *Revised Wechsler Intelligence Scale for Children (WISC-R), the VMI,* and the *VMI* supplemental tests for 17 children between the ages of 6 and 12 years of age who were identified in 1996 as having learning disabilities.

Table 10 Raw Score Correlations between the VMI and WISC-R (Decimals Omitted)			
	VMI	Visual	Motor
WISC Verbal IQ	48	43	41
WISC Performance IQ	66	58	55
WISC Full IQ	62	54	51

In earlier studies, the *VMI* correlated with mental age on the *Primary Mental Abilities* test at .59 for the first grade, .37 for fourth grade, and .38 for seventh grade (8). *VMI* correlations with *WISC-R* IQs were .49 for Verbal, .56 for Performance, and .56 for Full Scale with 93 students between 6 and 11 years of age (29). The *VMI* correlated .50 with *Slosson* IQs (39). Correlations between the *Stanford-Binet-Suzuki* and the *VMI* among Japanese children ages 11 to 15 ranged from .38 to .45 (186,187). With elderly psychiatric outpatients, the *VMI* has significantly correlated with the *WAIS-R* IQ scores as follows: Verbal .64, Performance .70, and Full Scale .68. (49).

Although the *VMI* correlates with intelligence, it correlates even more highly with chronological age and it appears to be a more sensitive index than intelligence for at least some physiological/neuropsychological problems in child development (5). General intelligence appears to be mediated more by the frontal, association areas of the cortex than visual-motor integration, which may be mediated more by white matter and other subcortical portions of the nervous system (154).

Hypothesis 5: Academic Achievement The abilities measured by the *VMI* and its supplemental tests are related to academic achievement. Thus, it was hypothesized that results from the tests will correlate moderately well with academic achievement test results. Table 11 shows 1996 correlations between the *Comprehensive Test of Basic Skills (CTBS)* and the *VMI* tests from 44 4th and 5th grade students from regular classrooms.

Table 11 Raw Score Correlations between the VMI and CTBS (Decimals Omitted)			
	VMI	Visual	Motor
CTBS Reading Total	58	31	31
CTBS Language Total	68	20	39
CTBS Mathematics Total	42	21	37
CTBS Overall Total	63	29	40

Prior to 1996, correlations between the *VMI* and readiness tests have averaged about .50 (23,107,143,166). Similarly, correlations between form copying and early reading achievement have generally ranged from about .40 to .60 (113, 142,150). Correlations with reading and other achievement tests have tended to be higher for the primary grades than the upper grades (23), with a tendency for the *VMI* to correlate more highly with arithmetic than with reading (173). Not all studies have found strong relationships (47,95,135,199). However, even at the graduate school level, correlations of .37 with arithmetic and .25 with penmanship have been reported (173).

Interculturally, *VMI* correlations have ranged from .51 to .73 for reading and mathematics among fifth and sixth grade Taiwanese children (111,112). They have ranged from .42 to .55 for reading and from .65 to .67 for mathematics among Japanese children 11 to 15 years old (186,187).

Factor analytic studies have indicated that visual-motor integration was the underlying, key factor for handwriting performance (168). For all age groups, the average correlation between the *VMI* and handwriting was .42, higher than correlations between handwriting and any of several other measures, including general intelligence, finger dexterity, and visual perception. Similar findings have been reported by others (118,177,189,193).

Hypothesis 6: Item and Person Separations The test items of the *VMI* and its supplemental tests measure similar respective traits and are effective in measuring persons. Thus, the Rasch-Wright item and person separation indices will be high, as shown in Table 4 on page 106.

Hypothesis 7: Disabling Conditions The abilities measured by the *VMI* are sensitive to certain disabling conditions. Thus, it is hypothesized that *VMI* results will be lower among such populations.

Brain-injured, educable mentally retarded, and partially-sighted children have done less well on the *VMI* than their peers (99,109,113). No differences were found between children with delayed language and those with normal language development (72). *VMI* scores of low academic achievers were not significantly different from children with learning disabilities (200). Apparently, poor visual-motor integration can result from slow maturation, inadequate educational experiences, socioeconomic deprivation and/or neurological and other physical problems. Rourke's hypotheses suggest that any significant interference in the development or maintenance of neural white matter, particularly the long associational fibers, may seriously disrupt intermodal integration and other important nervous system functions (154).

Significantly lowered *VMI* scores have been found to be characteristic of low birth weight children at various ages of follow up (74,133,149,185,202). It is extremely encouraging to see that early help for these children and their families seems to be very effective in increasing their development in a number of important ways, including visual-motor integration (26).

Another rather consistent finding has been that children with myelomeningocele (spina bifida) typically perform in the average range on visual perception tests, but perform significantly less well on the *VMI* (57,196). A similar, but less pronounced, pattern was found with lipomyelomeningocele (58).

Using the *VMI*, impaired visual-motor integration has been reported for preschool children with iron deficiency

(114), environmental exposure to lead (5,197), fetal alcohol syndrome(84), phenytoin and other anticonvulsant exposure (182), leukemia (89,117,126), cardiac arrest (127), Ullrich-Turner syndrome (152) and other serious medical problems (119,164).

Baghurst and others followed nearly 500 children during their first 7 years of life in order to assess the effects of exposure to environmental lead. On the basis of periodic blood samples and other tests, they found an inverse relation between the *VMI* and blood lead concentration. They concluded that the *VMI* appeared to be a more sensitive index for the assessment of lead effects on child development than global neuropsychological measures such as intelligence (5).

Comparisons of the *VMI* with tests of psycholinguistic abilities indicated that the *VMI* measures an integrative ability important to adequate functioning beyond visual-motor behavior. The *VMI* correlated highly with automatic-sequential subtests of the *Illinois Test of Psycholinguistic Abilities* and only moderately with the subtests designed to measure less integrative skills (8). Commonly, children with learning disabilities have displayed difficulty with such integration tasks (6).

Lyon and others (116) reported the *VMI* to be an effective measure for differentiating subtypes of reading disabilities. Their factor analytic neuropsychological work is provocative and may redirect productive future attention to psycholinguistic processes.

Factor analysis Polumbinski and others have tentatively defined four factors, or stages of development, in the *VMI* (140). The closed forms with acute and oblique angles accounted for the largest amount of variance (25%) in *VMI* performance. Other factor analytic studies found the *VMI* to fit well into a visuospatial-motor factor (195).

Predictive Validity

Generally, researchers have found the *VMI* to be a valuable predictor when used in combination with other measures (23,42,45,51,53,93,188). Comparison of a battery of pre-kindergarten test scores with the same children's achievement at the end of kindergarten and at the end of first grade indicated that the *VMI*, in combination with a test of auditory-vocal association, best predicted achievement (179). The *VMI* was particularly able to identify high-risk boys in kindergarten who subsequently had reading difficulty (159).

Reynolds and others (148) found that the *VMI* and the *Test for Auditory Comprehension of Language* both significantly predicted *SRA* Reading, Language Arts, and Mathematics between entering kindergarten and the end of first grade. Combining the two tests increased the accuracy of prediction only slightly.

LaTorre (104) confirmed Gates' finding that the *VMI*, as a part of the *Florida Kindergarten Screening Test*, predicted school achievement (59). Fletcher and Satz (52) found that inclusion of the *VMI* with three other brief tests correctly predicted 85% of kindergarten children who were problem readers seven years later. In the sixth grade, when the children were classified by reading achievement as severe problem, mild problem, average, or superior, it was found that their kindergarten *VMI* scores corresponded to these classifications.

VMI results, particularly when coupled with pediatrician's ratings, have been significantly predictive of school grade failures, or retentions (54). Similarly *VMI* results coupled with predictive ratings by kindergarten teachers have been effective in predicting second grade reading and were about as effective in prediction as the *K-ABC*. The *K-ABC* and similar instruments are much more expensive than the *VMI* as screening instruments because they must be individually administered by a specialist (120).

Visual-motor predictive correlations appear to decline as children move up the grade levels (93,178). One reason for this decline may be instructional shifts from visual-spatial skills, such as printing, to more language-based skills as grade levels increase (81). Also, many children learn to compensate for weaknesses by using other skills. At what price? Rourke has reported that children's personalities are significantly affected by non-verbal learning disabilities (154). Would these children achieve more fully, or at least more easily, if their visual-motor weaknesses were remediated? If so, how can such weaknesses best be remediated? These questions require further research.

Research on the *Bender-Gestalt* as a predictor of academic achievement has been summarized as contradictory (34). Other than the *VMI*, more recent tests of visual-motor ability have not reported any predictive validity studies.

Controlling for Bias

An important aspect of construct validity is evidence to show what a test is hypothesized *not* to be. It is hypothesized that the *VMI* and its supplemental tests are not biased with regard to gender, ethnicity, socioeconomic status, and residence. This hypothesis was supported by means of analysis of variance for the entire 1996 norming sample, as no statistically significant differences at the .05 level were found among the foregoing variables. Earlier evidence regarding bias includes:

Gender No statistically significant differences at the .05 level were found between female and male performances in the 1981 *VMI* norming studies. Although gender differences have been reported (66), the preponderance of studies have found no significant gender differences (4,130,143,159,167).

Ethnicity At early ages, Chinese children have performed somewhat better than U.S. children, but the norms were very similar from ages 9 to 17 (111,112). Greek (61) and Norwegian (168) children have performed slightly less well than U.S. children. No significant *VMI* differences have been found between Native American and non-Native American kindergarten children (143). Statistically significant differences between African-American and Caucasian children have been reported (130), but the opposite finding has also been obtained (161).

It is important to remember that *statistical* significance and *practical* significance can be very different, especially when large samples are involved. Very small differences can become statistically significant when large groups are studied. Nye, for example, reported a statistically significant difference between the *VMI* scores of a large sample of 3,766 African-American and Caucasian children in Head Start programs (130). However, only about 1% of the variance among the scores could be attributed to ethnicity.

The 1981 *VMI* norming studies, with another large sample of 2,060 children, produced similar results. Statistically significant differences were found among children of African-American, Caucasian, Hispanic-American, and other ethnic groups. However, almost all of the score variance was attributable to chronological age, with less than 1% of the variance due to ethnicity (9). Especially compared to many other types of tests, the *VMI* appears to be essentially culture free.

Socioeconomic Status The 1981 *VMI* norming study, employing a very large sample, found a statistically significant difference between the scores of children whose families had annual incomes below and above the poverty level. However, only about 3% of the variance in *VMI* scores was attributable to income level (9). Although differences on the *VMI* among very large samples of socioeconomic groups were reported by Nye (130), other studies have not found such differences (23,29).

Residence No statistically significant differences at the .05 level were found among rural, urban, and suburban children's performances in the 1964 *VMI* norming studies (8). Although, for a very large sample, a statistically significant difference in favor of rural and urban scores over those from mixed rural-urban populations was reported, no significant differences were found between rural and urban Head Start children's *VMI* scores (130).

VIII. Teaching

In the original *VMI* Manual, a diagnostic teaching strategy was provided to help identify which sub-skills of visual-motor integration might need remediation with a given child. The basic strategy was to *test down* a sequence of *VMI* sub-skills, from most to least complex, and to *teach up* the sub-skills sequence from the point at which a child first encountered difficulty. This *test down and teach up* strategy, which is still very useful for diagnostic-remedial purposes, is reflected in the testing procedures entitled *Testing the Limits* on pages 29-30.

A number of studies report significant improvements in *VMI* test scores and similar sensory-motor measures following various types of teaching programs (33,44). However, transfer of improved sensory-motor integration skills to academic skills does not occur automatically (125,145). Thus, effective processes for teaching children to draw circles and squares need to be applied, as soon as children are ready, to the teaching of letters, words, sentences, and other shapes. Difficulty in learning to print and write is frequently a sign of learning disability (154). Therefore, this teaching section summarizes the basic concepts and practices for evaluating and teaching handwriting which are utilized in the *Integrated Writing Test* and the *Integrated Writing* teaching materials which the author has developed (17,18,68,77,82,102,121).

Handwriting

Besides the fact that handwriting, as a common graphic behavior, is a natural vehicle for teaching, there are broader reasons for focusing upon it. Our schools are encountering increasing numbers of children who lack solid mental and social foundations, who are at risk of becoming school and social dropouts.

Handwriting is frequently an indicator of children's mental and social foundations. If a child lacks an adequate mental foundation, in the Piagetian sense, because of insufficient sensory-motor and other experiences, it tends to show up in poor handwriting. Similarly, if a child lacks an adequate social foundation – has not developed basic self-respect and respect for others – it also tends to be evidenced in poor handwriting.

Because it is so visible (in contrast to spoken language), poor handwriting often operates as a self-fulfilling prophesy. If a child is allowed to continuously portray his mental and social inadequacies graphically, he may come to increasingly believe that he is an inferior person and to behave accordingly.

On the other hand, a child who is taught to consistently write well not only strengthens her or his sensory-motor foundations, but also receives continuous, powerful reinforcement for development of a positive self-concept, self-discipline, effort, pride in accomplishment, and mutual respect.

When?

Keeping in mind Piaget's and others' developmental findings, it seems prudent to postpone formal pencil and paper writing at least until a child can easily execute a copy of the *VMI* Oblique Cross. The Oblique Cross requires the ability to draw the diagonal lines used in many letters. It also requires crossing the child's midline, which is the source of many (if not most) reversal problems. Pencil work needs to be preceded by gross motor and other large muscle experiences, such as painting (102).

What?

What are important components of a good preventative and remedial handwriting program? They include the following:

Shape Curlicues, slants, and other expressions of taste need to be postponed until children clearly and consistently demonstrate mastery of simple letter shapes. Slants and other embellishments can be easily added later.

Use of manuscript or a continuous-stroke script for early writers is still controversial. Some believe that manuscript, with its frequent stroke starts and stops, is too difficult for early writers and remedial pupils. Others believe the opposite. Research has produced mixed results (68). At one point in time, the *VMI* author thought that continuous strokes with *tails* at their ends were desirable, at least from the standpoint of easy transition to cursive. However, further experience has suggested that the slants and tails of some alphabets complicate, rather than help, many early and remedial writing efforts.

Size One of the most fundamental child-development teaching principles is to *work from large to small.* It is important to remember that children are normally far-sighted until third or fourth grade, and their eyes do not reach adult size and shape until about age 10. Some handwriting programs require early writers to use .5" lines, allowing only .25" for lower-case letters. Writing lines that are too small create fatigue and frustration which can generalize beyond handwriting into negative attitudes towards school, learning, self, and others.

Good teaching of handwriting begins with chalkboard and other large-muscle work and gradually becomes refined. Handwriting worksheets – throughout the elementary grades – should include lines of *varying* sizes, up to 1" high or more, to help pupils learn to use their *arms,* not just their fingers.

Tracing All major handwriting programs correctly provide a good deal of tracing as well as copying exercise. However, they rarely provide tracing stimuli that give the child and teacher clear feedback. Some programs use solid tracing stimuli, which do not allow the child or teacher to see the tracing marks. Other programs use dashes or shaded stimuli, which are little better. Handwriting worksheets need to provide letters with pathways like those used in the *VMI's Motor Coordination* tests (18).

Content Teaching time is precious. While students are learning and practicing good handwriting, the content of what they write should be as valuable as possible. Research indicates that the development of respect for one's self and for others is basic to success in school and in later life (16). Some handwriting content should probably focus on the development of mutual respect.

Evaluation Emphasis upon self-evaluation is a powerful teaching tool in almost any area of curriculum, including handwriting. Daily handwriting lessons should frequently include some form of self-evaluation, ranging from merely circling one's best work on a line to writing compositions about how well one is progressing in handwriting and/or other other areas, such as mutual respect. An objectified self-evaluation of letter formation and other aspects of writing should also be periodically administered and reported to students.

All of the foregoing principles and practices, from pre-handwriting readiness to advanced aspects of content and composition, have been implemented in the *Integrated Writing Test* and in its accompanying teaching materials (17,18).

Bibliography and References

1. American Educational Research Association, American Psychological Association, & National Council on Measurement in Education. *Standards for educational and psychological testing.* Washington, DC: American Psychological Association, 1985.

2. Anastasi, A. *Psychological testing (6th ed.).* NYC: Macmillan, 1988.

3. Armstrong, B.B., & Knopf, K.F. Comparison of the Bender-Gestalt and Revised Developmental Test of Visual-Motor Integration. *Perceptual & Motor Skills,* 55, 164-166, 1982.

4. Aylward, E.H., & Schmidt, S. An examination of three tests of visual-motor integration. *Journal of Learning Disabilities,* 19, 328-330, 1986.

5. Baghurst, P.A., McMichael, A.J., Tong S., Wigg, N.R., Vimpani, G.V., & Robertson, E.F. Exposure to environmental lead and visual-motor integration at age 7 years: the Port Pirie Cohort Study. *Epidemiology,* 6, 2, 104-109, 1995.

6. Bateman, B.D. Learning disorders. *Review of Educational Research,* 36, 93-119, 1966.

7. Bayley, N. *Bayley Scales of Infant Development (2nd Ed.).* San Antonio, TX: The Psychological Corporation, 1993.

8. Beery, K.E. *Visual-motor integration monograph.* Chicago, IL: Follett Publishing Company, 1967.

9. Beery, K.E. *The Developmental Test of Visual-Motor Integration.* Cleveland, OH: Modern Curriculum Press, 1967, 1982, 1989.

10. Beery, K.E. Estimation of Angles. *Perceptual & Motor Skills,* 26, 11, 1968.

11. Beery, K.E. Form Reproduction as a Function of Angularity, Orientation, Brightness, Contrast, and Hue. *Perceptual & Motor Skills,* 26, 235-243, 1968.

12. Beery, K.E. Form Reproduction as a Function of Complexity. *Perceptual & Motor Skills,* 26, 219-222, 1968.

13. Beery, K.E. Integration as a Factor in Psycholinguistic Performance. *Perceptual & Motor Skills,* 26, 284, 1968.

14. Beery, K.E. Comprehensive research, evaluation, and assistance for exceptional children. *Exceptional Children,* 35, 223-228, 1968.

15. Beery, K.E. *Models for Mainstreaming.* Sioux Falls, SD: Adapt Press, 1972.

16. Beery, K.E. *Respect: The first "R" on report cards.* Novato, CA: Academic Therapy Publications, 1987.

17. Beery, K.E. *Integrated Writing Test.* Redding, CA: Golden Educational Center, 1993.

18. Beery, K.E., & McEowen, S.L. *Integrated Writing.* Redding, CA: Golden Educational Center, 1993.

19. Bender, L. *A visual motor gestalt test and its clinical use. Research Monograph Number 3.* NYC: American Orthopsychiatric Association, 1938.

20. Birch, H.G., & Lefford, A. Intersensory development in children. *Society for Research in Child Development Monographs,* 28, 5, 1963.

21. Braken, B.A. The interpretation of tests. In Zeidner, M., & Most, R. (Eds.) *Psychological testing: An inside view.* Palo Alto: Consulting Psychologists Press, 1992.

22. Brand, H.J. Correlation for scores on Revised Test of Visual-Motor Integration and Copying Test in a South African sample. *Perceptual and Motor Skills,* 73, 1, 225-226, 1991.

23. Bray, B.M. The relationships between tests of visual-motor integration, aptitude, and achievement among first-grade children. Master's thesis, Bryn Mawr College Graduate School, May, 1974.

24. Breen, M.J. Comparison of educationally handicapped students' scores on the revised Developmental Test of Visual-Motor Integration and Bender-Gestalt. *Perceptual & Motor Skills,* 54, 1127-1130, 1982.

25. Breen, M.J., Carlson, M., & Lehman, J. The Revised Developmental Test of Visual-Motor Integration: Its relation to the VMI, WISC-R, and Bender Gestalt for a group of elementary aged learning disabled students. *Journal of Learning Disabilities,* 18, 196-198, 1985.

26. Brooks-Gunn, J., Liaw, F.R., & Klebanov, P.K. Effects of early intervention on cognitive function of low birth weight preterm infants. *Journal of Pediatrics,* Mar, 120, 3, 350-9, 1992.

27. Brown, M.J. Comparison of the Developmental Test of Visual-Motor Integration and the Bender-Gestalt test. *Perceptual & Motor Skills,* 45, 3, (Pt 1), 981-982, 1977.

28. Bruner, J.S. The course of cognitive growth. *American Psychologist,* 19, 1-15, 1964.

29. Buktenica, N.A. Relative contributions of auditory and visual perception to first-grade language learning. Doctoral dissertation, University of Chicago, 1966.

30. Buktenica, N.A. Identification of potential learning disorders. *Journal of Learning Disabilities,* 4, 379-383, 1971.

31. Carlson, L.A. *The nexus: test results to insights for remediation.* Novato, CA: Academic Therapy Publications, 1978.

32. Cattell, T. *The measurement of intelligence of infants and young children.* Revised Ed. NYC: Psychological Corporation, 1960.

33. Clark, C.M., & Dodd, B.E. Auditory factor in visual-motor testing and training. *Journal of Learning Disabilities,* 4: 582-85, 1971.

34. Compton, C. *A guide to 100 tests for special education.* Upper Saddle River, NJ: Globe Fearon Educational Publisher, 1996.

35. Connelly, J.B. Comparative analysis of two tests of visual-motor integration among young Indian and non-Indian children. *Perceptual & Motor Skills,* 57, 1079-1082, 1983.

36. Cratty, B.J. *Perceptual and motor development in infants and children.* Inglewood Cliffs, NJ: Prentice-Hall, 1979.

37. Crofoot, M.J., & Bennett, T.S. A comparison of three screening tests and the WISC-R in special education evaluations. *Psychology in the Schools,* 17, 474-478, 1980.

38. Curtis, C.J., Michael, J.J., & Michael, W.B. The Predictive Validity of the Developmental Test of Visual-Motor Integration under group and individual modes of administration relative to academic performance measures of second-grade pupils without identifiable major learning disabilities. *Educational & Psychological Measurement,* 39, 401-410, 1979.

39. De Mers, S.T., et al. Comparison of scores on two visual-motor tests for children referred for learning adjustment difficulties. *Perceptual & Motor Skills,* 53, 863-867, 1981.

40. Deutsch, M., et al. Guidelines for testing minority group children. *Journal of Social Issues* 20, 129-145, 1964.

41. Di Stefano, M., Sauerwein, H.C., & Lassonde, M. Influence of anatomical factors and spatial compatibility on the stimulus-response relationship in the absence of the corpus callosum. *Neuropsychologia,* 30, 2, 177-185, 1992 .

42. DiBacco, J.P. The efficacy of group and individually administered perceptual tests in predicting multicriteria first grade achievement. Doctoral dissertation, Peabody College, 1975. *Dissertation Abstracts International,* 37 (7536A), 1975.

43. Dick, R., Arnold, E., & Lessler, K. Preschool screening in North Carolina. A paper prepared for the North Carolina Office of Comprehensive Health Planning. Chapel Hill, NC: Human Resource Consultants, 1971.

44. Dickerson, J.N. A study of the effectiveness of a non-specialist in remediating visual-motor skills in a Title I school. South Bend, IN: South Bend Community School Corporation, 1972.

45. Duffy, F.B., Ritter, D.R., & Fedner, M. Developmental Test of Visual-Motor Integration and the Goodenough Draw-A-Man test as predictors of academic success. *Perceptual & Motor Skills*, 43, 543-546, 1976.

46. Elizabeth, H.A., & Stevens, S. An examination of three tests of visual-motor integration. *Journal of Learning Disabilities*, 19, 328-330, 1986.

47. Elkins, J., et al. Multivariate relationships between cognitive and reading measures in third-grade children. *Exceptional Child*, 24, 65-72, 1977.

48. Enstrom, E.A., & Enstrom, D.C. Solving early reading problems via handwriting. In Arena, J. (Ed.) *Building handwriting skills*. Novato, CA: Academic Therapy Publications, 1970.

49. Ferere, H., Burns, W.J., & Roth, L. Use of the Revised Developmental Test of Visual-Motor Integration with chronic mentally ill adult population. *Perceptual & Motor Skills*, 74, 1, 287-290, 1992.

50. Fernald, G. *Remedial techniques in basic school subjects*. NYC: McGraw-Hill, 1943.

51. Fletcher, J.M., & Satz, P. Developmental changes in the neuropsychological correlates of reading achievement: a six-year longitudinal followup. *Journal of Clinical Neuropsychology*, 2, 23-37, 1980.

52. Fletcher, J.M., & Satz, P. Kindergarten prediction of reading achievement: a seven-year longitudinal follow-up. *Educational & Psychological Measurement*, 42, 681-685, 1982.

53. Flynn, T.M., & Flynn, L.A. Evaluation of the predictive ability of five screening measures administered during kindergarten. *Journal of Experimental Education*, 46, 65-70, 1978.

54. Fowler, M.G., & Cross, A.W. Preschool risk factors as predictors of early school performance. *Journal of Developmental & Behavioral Pediatrics*, 7, 4, 237-241, 1986 .

55. Frey, P.D., & Pinelli, B. Visual discrimination and visuomotor integration among two classes of Brazilian children. *Perceptual & Motor Skills*, 72, 3, (Pt 1), 847-850, 1991.

56. Friedman, et al. A brief screening battery for predicting school achievement at ages seven and nine years. *Psychology in the Schools*, 17, 340-346, 1980.

57. Friedrich, W.N., Lovejoy, M.C., Shaffer, J., Shurtleff, D.B., and others. Cognitive abilities and achievement status of children with myelomeningocels: a contemporary sample. *Journal of Pediatric Psychology*, 16, 4, 423-428, 1991.

58. Friedrich, W.N., Shurtleff, D.B., & Shaffer, J. Cognitive abilities and lipomyelomeningocele. *Psychological Reports*, 73, 2, 467-470, 1993.

59. Gates, R.D. Florida Kindergarten Screening Battery. *Journal of Clinical Neuropsychology*, 6, 459-465, 1984.

60. Georgas, J.G., & Papadopoulou, E. The Harris-Goodenough and the Developmental Form Sequence (VMI) with five-year-old Greek children. *Perceptual & Motor Skills*, 26, 352-354, 1968.

61. Georgas, J.G. *The Georgas Test*. Athens, Greece: KEPO, 1971.

62. Gerard, J.A., & Junkala, J. Task analysis, handwriting, and process-based instruction. *Journal of Learning Disabilities*, 13, 49-53, 1980.

63. Gesell, A., et al. *Yale University clinic of child development: the first five years of life*. NYC: Harper, 1940.

64. Gesell, A. *Developmental Schedules*. NYC: Psychological Corporation, 1956.

65. Glanville, J.T. Reliability study using Beery-Buktenica Developmental Form Sequence (VMI) with emotionally disturbed-socially maladjusted children. Master's thesis. University of Kansas, 1968.

66. Gotthold, J., & Weinstein, D.J. A correlation of the Bender-Gestalt test and the Beery Developmental Test of Visual-Motor Integration. Unpublished master's thesis. Case Western University, 1975.

67. Grafton, S.T., Mazziotta, J.C., Woods, R.P., & Phelps, M.E. Human functional anatomy of visually guided finger movements. *Brain*, 115, 2, 565-587, 1992.

68. Graham, S., & Miller, L. Handwriting research and practice: a unified approach. *Focus on Exceptional Children*, 13, 2, 1980.

69. Grant, M.L., Ilai, D., Nussbaum, N.L., & Bigler, E.D. The relationship between continuous performance tasks and neuropsychological tests in children with Attention-deficit Hyperactivity Disorder. *Perceptual & Motor Skills*, 70, 2, 1990.

70. Griffiths, R. *The abilities of babies*. NYC: McGraw-Hill, 1954.

71. Gunderson, B. Diagnosis of learning disabilities-the team approach. *Journal of Learning Disabilities*, 4, 107-113, 1971.

72. Halloway, G.F. Auditory-visual integration in language delayed children. *Journal of Learning Disabilities*, 4, 204-208, 1971.

73. Halsband, U., & Homberg, V. Hemispheric specialization in visual, tactile and crossmodal assembling tasks. *Cortex*, 26, 4, 625-637, 1990.

74. Halsey, C.L., Collin, M.F., & Anderson, C.L. Extremely low birth weight children and their peers: a comparison of preschool performance. *Pediatrics*, 91, 4, 807-811, 1993.

75. Halstead, W.C. *Brain and Intelligence*. Chicago: University of Chicago Press, 1947

76. Hammer, A.L. Test evaluation and quality. In Zeidner, M., & Most, R. *Psychological testing: An inside view.* Palo Alto, CA: Consulting Psychologists Press, Inc., 1992.

77. Hammill, D.D., & Bartell, N.R. *Teaching students with learning and behavior problems.* Austin,TX: Pro-Ed, 1995.

78. Hammill, D.D., Pearson, N.A., & Voress, J.K. *Developmental Tests of Visual Perception (2nd Ed.).* Austin, TX: Pro-Ed, 1993.

79. Haring, N.G., & Bateman, B.D. *Teaching the learning disabled child.* Englewood Cliffs, NJ: Prentice-Hall, 1977.

80. Hartlage, L.C., & Lucas, T.L. Differential correlates of Bender-Gestalt and Beery visual-motor integration test for black and white children. *Perceptual & Motor Skills,* 43, 1039-1042, 1976.

81. Hartlage, Lawrence C., & Golden, Charles J. Neuropsychological assessment techniques. In *The handbook of school psychology (2nd ed.).* Gutkin, T.B., & Reynolds, C.R. (Eds.). NYC: John Wiley & Sons, 431-445, 1990.

82. Hofmeister, A.M. *Handwriting resource book.* Texas: DLM, 1981.

83. Hunt, J.McV. *Intelligence and experience.* NYC: Ronald Press, 1961.

84. Janzen, L.A., Nanson, J.L., & Block, G.W. Neuropsychological evaluation of preschoolers with fetal alcohol syndrome. *School Psychology International,* 4, 3, 129-140, 1983.

85. Junior, B.P., & Pasquali, L. Validacao do teste do desenvolvimento da integracao viso-motora (VMI), para uso no Brasil. Validation of the developmental test of visual-motor integration (VMI) for use in Brazil. *Psicologia,* Teoria e Pesquisa, Ma, 1992.

86. Kaufman, H.S., & Biven, P.L. Cursive writing: an aid to reading and spelling. *Academic Therapy,* 15, 209-19, 1979.

87. Kellogg, R. *Analyzing children's art.* Palo Alto, CA: Mayfield, 1970.

88. Kephart, N.C. *The slow learner in the classroom.* Columbus, OH: Charles Merrill, 1960.

89. Kingma, A., Mooyaart, E.L., Kamps, W.A., Nieuwenhuizen, P., & Wilmink, J.T. Magnetic resonance imaging of the brain and neuropsychological evaluation in children treated for acute lymphoblastic leukemia at a young age. *American Journal of Pediatric Hematology/Oncology,* 15, 2, 231-238, 1993.

90. Kirk, A., & Kertesz, A. Subcortical contributions to drawing. *Brain and Cognition,* 21, 1, 57-70, 1993.

91. Kirk, S.A. & McCarthy, J.J. The Illinois Test of Psycholinguistic Abilities. *American Journal of Mental Deficiency,* 66, 399-412, 1961.

92. Kirkham, E.K. *The handwriting of American records for a period of 300 years.* Logan, UT: Everton Publishers, 1973.

93. Klein, A.E. The validity of the Beery test of visual-motor integration in predicting achievement in kindergarten, first, and second grades. *Educational & Psychological Measurement*, 38, 457-61, 1978.

94. Kleinman, B.L., & Stalcup, A. The effect of graded craft activities on visuomotor integration in an inpatient child psychiatry population. *American Journal of Occupational Therapy*, 45, 4, 324-330, 1991.

95. Knoff, H.M., et al. Differential effectiveness of receptive language and visual-motor assessments in identifying academically gifted elementary school students. *Perceptual & Motor Skills*, 63, 719-725, 1986.

96. Knoff, H.M., & Sperling, B.L. Gifted children and visual-motor development: A comparison of Bender-Gestalt and VMI test performance. *Psychology in the Schools*, 23, 3, 247-251, 1986.

97. Koppitz, E.M. *The Bender-Gestalt test for young children.* NYC: Grune and Stratton, 1964.

98. Koppitz, E.M. *The Bender-Gestalt test for young children, vol. 2.* NYC: Grune and Stratton, 1975.

99. Kraetcsh-Heller, G. Use of the Beery visual-motor integration test with partially sighted students. *Perceptual & Motor Skills*, 43, 11-14, 1976.

100. Krauft, V.C., & Krauft, C.C. Structured vs. unstructured visual-motor test for educable retarded children. *Perceptual & Motor Skills*, 34, 691-694, 1972.

101. Kucia, M.M. *Phonics.* Cleveland, OH: Modern Curriculum Press, 1988.

102. Lamme, L.L. Handwriting in early childhood curricula. *Young Children*, 35, 20-27, 1979.

103. Lassonde, M., Sauerwein, H.C., & Lepore, F. Extent and limits of callosal plasticity: presence of disconnection symptoms in callosal agenesis. *Neuropsychologia*, 33, 8, 989-1007, 1995.

104. LaTorre, R.A. Kindergarten screening: A cross-validation of the Florida Kindergarten Screening Battery. *Alberta Journal of Educational Research*, 31, 174-190, 1985.

105. Lehman, J., & Breen, M.J. A comparative analysis of the Bender-Gestalt and Beery- Buktenica tests of visual-motor integration as a function of grade level for regular education students. *Psychology in the Schools*, 19, 52-54, 1982.

106. Lepkin, S.R., & Pryzwansky, W. Interrater reliability of the original and a revised scoring system for the developmental test of visual-motor integration. *Psychology in the Schools*, 20, 284-288, 1983.

107. Leton, D.A. A factor analysis of readiness tests. *Perceptual & Motor Skills*, 16, 915-919, 1963.

108. Levy, D.L., & Ellis, W. A clinical model for treatment of dyslexia. *Annals of Dyslexia,* 34, 285-296, 1984.

109. Liemohn, W., & Wagner, P. Motor and perceptual determinants of performance on the Bender-Gestalt and the Beery developmental scale by retarded males. *Perceptual & Motor Skills,* 40, 524-526, 1975.

110. Liemohn, W. Rhythm and motor ability in developmentally disabled children. *ERIC* #107637, 1975.

111. Liu Hung-Hsiang. *A revision of Beery's developmental test of visual-motor integration.* Taipei, Taiwan: Provincial Taipei Junior Normal College, 1972.

112. Liu, Hung-Hsiang. *A Report on the Revision of the Beery Developmental Test of Visual Motor Integration.* National Taipei Teachers College, Taipei, Taiwan, Republic of China, 1991.

113. Lowder, R.C. *Perceptual ability and school achievement.* Winter Haven, FL: Winter Haven Lions Club, 1966.

114. Lozoff, B., Jimenez, E., & Wolf, A.W. Long-term developmental outcome of infants with iron deficiency. *New England Journal of Medicine,* 325, 10, 687-694, 1991.

115. Luria, A.R. *The working brain.* NYC: Basic Books, 1973.

116. Lyon, R., et al. Neuropsychological characteristics of empirically derived subgroups of learning disabled readers. *Journal of Clinical Neuropsychology,* 4, 343-365, 1982.

117. MacLean, W.E., Jr., Noll, R.B., Stehbens, J.A., Kaleita, T.A., Schwartz, E., Whitt, J.K., Cantor, N.L., Waskerwitz, M., Ruymann, F., & Novak. L.J., et al. Neuropsychological effects of cranial irradiation in young children with acute lymphoblastic leukemia 9 months after diagnosis. *Archives of Neurology,* 52, 2, 156-160, 1995.

118. Maeland, A.F. Handwriting and perceptual-motor skills in clumsy, dysgraphic, and 'normal' children. *Perceptual and Motor Skills,* 75, 3 (Pt 2), 1207-1217, 1992.

119. Majnemer, A., & Rosenblatt, B. Prediction of outcome at school entry in neonatal intensive care unit survivors, with use of clinical and electrophysiologic techniques. *Journal of Pediatrics,* 127, 5, 823-830, 1995.

120. Mantzicopoulos, P.Y., & Morrison, D. Early prediction of reading achievement: Exploring the relationship of cognitive and noncognitive measures to inaccurate classifications of at-risk status. *RASE: Remedial & Special Education,* 15, 1994.

121. Martin, J.H. Writing to read. Boca Raton, FL: IBM Education, 1986.

122. Martin, R., Sewell, T., & Manni, J. Effects of race and social class on preschool performance on the Developmental Test of Visual-Motor Integration. *Psychology in the Schools,* 14, 4, 466-470, 1977.

123. Melamed, L.E., & Melamed, E.C. Neurop*sychology of perception*. In Hartlage, L.C., & Telzrow, C.F. (Eds.). *The neuropsychology of individual differences*. NYC: Plenum, 1985.

124. Miccinati, J. Teach reading disabled students to perceive distinct features in words. *Journal of Learning Disabilities*, 14, 140-142, 1981.

125. Montessori, M. *Dr. Montessori's own handbook*. NYC: Schocken, 1965.

126. Moore, I.M., Kramer, J.H., Wara, W., Halberg, F., & Ablin, A.R. Cognitive function in children with leukemia. Effect of radiation dose and time since irradiation. *Cancer*, 68, 9, 1913-1917, 1991.

127. Morris, R.D., Krawiecki, N.S., Wright, J.A., & Walter, L.W. Neuropsychological, academic, and adaptive functioning in children who survive in-hospital cardiac arrest and resuscitation. Special Series: Pediatric chronic illness. *Journal of Learning Disabilities*, 26, 1, 46-51, 1993.

128. Mullin, E.M. *Mullen Scales of Early Learning*. Circle Pines, MN: AGS, 1995.

129. Nelson, J.C., et al. *The Edmonton preschool screening project*. Edmonton, Alberta: University of Alberta, 1973.

130. Nye, B.A. A factorial analysis of variance and resulting norm tables for Tennessee Head Start children based on the Developmental Test of Visual-Motor Integration. *ERIC* #ED158879, 1977.

131. O'Donnell, P.A. *Motor & Haptic Learning*. Dimensions in Early Learning. Sioux Falls, SD: Adapt Press, 1969.

132. O'Donnell, P.A., & Eisenson, J. Delacato training for reading achievement and visual-motor integration. *Journal of Learning Disabilities*, 2, 441-447, 1969.

133. Ornstein, M., Ohlsson, A., Edmonds, J., & Asztalos, E. Neonatal follow-up of very low birthweight/extremely low birthweight infants to school age: a critical overview. *Acta Paediatrica Scandinavia*, 80, 8-9, 741-748, 1991.

134. Otto, W. Handwriting. *Encyclopedia of Educational Research, 4th Ed.* NYC: Macmillan, 1969.

135. Park, R. Performance on geometric figure copying tests as predictors of types of errors in decoding. *Reading Research Quarterly*, 1, 100-118, 1978.

136. Peck, M., et al. Another decade of research in handwriting: progress and prospect in the 1970's. *Journal of Educational Research*, 73, 283-298, 1980.

137. Pedersen, E., et al. A new perspective on the effects of first-grade teachers on children's subsequent adult status. *Harvard Educational Review*, 48, 1-31, 1978.

138. Piaget, J. *The origins of intelligence in children.* NYC: International Universities Press, 1952.

139. Picard, E.M., & Rourke, B.P. Neuropsychological consequences of prophylactic treatment of acute lymphocytic leukemia. In Rourke, B.P. (Ed.), *Syndrome of Nonverbal Learning Disabilities.* NYC: The Guilford Press, 1995.

140. Polumbinski, J., et al. Factor structure evidence for developmental levels of perceptual processing on the Developmental Test of Visual-Motor Integration. *Psychology in the Schools,* 23, 337-341, 1986.

141. Porter, G., & Binder, G.M. A pilot study of visual-motor developmental integration test reliability: the Beery Developmental Test of Visual-Motor Integration and the Bender-Gestalt test. *Journal of Learning Disabilities,* 14, 124-127, 1981.

142. Potter, M.C. *Perception of symbol orientation and early reading success.* NYC: Teachers' College, Columbia University, 1949.

143. Price, J.H. A validity study of the Pacific Infants Performance Scale involving kindergarten children. Doctoral dissertation, University of Wyoming, 1980.

144. Pryzwansky, W.B. The use of the Developmental Test of Visual-Motor Integration as a group screen instrument. *Psychology in the Schools,* 14, 419-422, 1977.

145. Quarmley, L.L. The effect of perceptual motor training on reading readiness of kindergarten children. Dissertation, Lehigh University, 1973.

146. Rand, C.W. Copying in drawing, the importance of adequate visual analysis versus the ability to use drawing rules. *Child Development,* 44, 47-52, 1973.

147. Reitan, R.M., & Davidson, L.A. (Eds.). *Clinical neuropsychology: Current status and applications.* Washington, DC: V.H. Winston, 1974.

148. Reynolds, C.R., et al. Incremental validity of the test for auditory comprehension of language and the Developmental Test of Visual-Motor Integration. *Educational & Psychological Measurement,* 40, 503-507, 1980.

149. Robertson, C.M., Etches, P.C., & Kyle, J.M. Eight-year school performance and growth of preterm, small for gestational age infants: a comparative study with subjects matched for birth weight or for gestational age. *Journal of Pediatrics,* 116, 1, 19-26, 1990.

150. Robinson, H., et al. An evaluation of the children's visual achievement forms at grade 1. *American Journal of Optometry,* 35, 515-525, 1958.

151. Rodger, S. A survey of assessments used by paediatric occupational therapists. *Australian Occupational Therapy Journal,* 41, 3, 137-142, 1994.

152. Ross, J.L., Stefanatos, G., Roeltgen, D., Kushner, H., & Cutler, G.B. Jr. Ullrich-Turner syndrome: neurodevelopmental changes from childhood through adolescence. *American Journal of Medical Genetics*, 58, 1, 74-82, 1995.

153. Roth, M.A., McCaul, E., & Barnes, K. Who Becomes an "At-Risk" Student? The Predictive Value of a Kindergarten Screen Battery. *Exceptional Children*, 59, 4, 348-358, 1993.

154. Rourke, B.P. (Ed.) *Syndrome of Nonverbal Learning Disabilities: Neurodevelopmental Manifestations*. NYC: The Guilford Press, 1995.

155. Ryckman, D.B., et al. Reliabilities of three tests of form-copying. *Perceptual & Motor Skills*, 34, 917-918, 1972.

156. Saigal, S., Szatmari, P., Rosenbaum, P., Campbell, D., & King, S. Cognitive abilities and school performance of extremely low birth weight children and matched term control children at age 8 years: a regional study. *Journal of Pediatrics*, May, 118, 5, 751-760, 1991.

157. Salvia, J., & Ysseldyke, J.E. *Assessment*. Boston: Houghton Mifflin Co., 1991.

158. Sattler, J.M. *Assessment of children*. San Diego, CA: Jerome M. Sattler, 1992.

159. Satz, P. & Friel, J. Some predictive antecedent of specific reading disability: a preliminary two-year follow-up. *Journal of Learning Disabilities*, 7, 48-55, 1974.

160. Schiller, R.A. The effect of differing format on two visual motor tests. Master's thesis, Case Western Reserve University, 1978.

161. Schooler, D.L., & Anderson, R.L. Race differences on the Developmental Test of Visual-Motor Integration, the Slosson intelligence test, and the ABC inventory. *Psychology in the Schools*, 16, 453-456, 1979.

162. Shapiro, Steven K., & Simpson, Robert G. Patterns and predictors of performance on the Bender-Gestalt and the Developmental Test of Visual Motor Integration in a sample of behaviorally and emotionally disturbed adolescents. *Journal of Psychoeducational Assessment*, 12, 3, 254-263, 1994.

163. Siewert, J.C., & Breen, M.J. The Revised Test of Visual-Motor Integration: its relation to the Test of Visual-Motor Integration and Bender Visual-Motor Gestalt Test for regular education students. *Psychology in the Schools*, 20, 304-306, 1983.

164. Silvestri, J.M., Weese-Mayer, D.E., & Nelson, M.N. Neuropsychologic abnormalities in children with congenital central hypoventilation syndrome. *Journal of Pediatrics*, 120, 3, 388-393, 1992.

165. Skeen, J.A., et al. Comparison of learning-disabled children's performance on the Bender Visual-Motor Gestalt Test and Beery's Developmental Test of Visual-Motor Integration. *Perceptual & Motor Skills,* 55, 1257-1258, 1982.

166. Small, V.H. Ocular pursuit abilities and readiness for reading. Dissertation, Purdue University, 1958.

167. Southworth, L.G. Predicting difficulty in first-grade reading from brief screening of kindergarten children with perceptual tasks. Dissertation, University of Tennessee, 1973.

168. Sovik, N. *Developmental cybernetics of handwriting and graphic behavior.* Oslo: Univesitetsforglaget, 1975.

169. Spirito, A. Scores on Bender-Gestalt and the Developmental Test of Visual-Motor Integration of learning-disabled children. *Perceptual & Motor Skills,* 50, 1214, 1980.

170. Starr, A. *The Rutgers Drawing Test.* The Training School Bulletin 49, 45-64, 1952.

171. Strauss, A.A., & Lehtinin, L. *Psychopathology and education of the brain-injured child.* NYC: Grune and Stratton, 1947.

172. Strauss, A.A., & Kephart, N.C. *Psychopathology and education of the brain-injured child.* NYC: Grune and Stratton, 1955.

173. Tarnopol, L., & Tarnopol, M. *Comparative reading and learning difficulties.* Lexington, MA: Lexington Books, 1981.

174. Terman, L.M., et al. *Stanford-Binet (L&M).* Boston: Houghton Mifflin, 1937.

175. Thompson, N.M., Fletcher, J.M., Chapiesk, L., Landry, S.H., Miner, M.E., & Bixby, J. Cognitive and motor abilities in preschool hydrocephalics. *Journal of Clinical and Experimental Neuropsychology,* 13, 2, 245-258, 1991.

176. Tolor, A., & Schulberg, H.C. *An evaluation of the Bender-Gestalt test.* Springfield, IL: Charles C. Thomas, 1963.

177. Tseng, M.H., & Murray, E.A. Differences in perceptual-motor measures in children with good and poor handwriting. *Occupational Therapy Journal of Research,* 14, 1, 19-36, 1994.

178. Tucker, R.E. The relationship between perceptual-motor development and academic achievement. Dissertation, University of Alabama, 1976.

179. *University City School District early education screening test battery of basic skills development.* University City, MO: University School District, 1969.

180. U.S. Department of Commerce, Bureau of the Census. *Census of Population: 1990. General Population Characteristics.* Washington, DC: U.S. Government Printing Office, 1992.

181. Van Leeuwen, H. M., & Slot, H. M. De coordinatie-ontwikkel-ingsstoornis: een nieuwe diagnostische categorie in de DSM-III/R. Developmental coordination disorder: A new diagnostic category in DSM-III-R Tijdschrift voor. *Psychiatrie, 33, 9,* 592-606, 1991.

182. Vanoverloop, D., Schnell, R.R., Harvey, E.A., & Holmes, L.B. The effects of prenatal exposure to phenytoin and other anticonvulsants on intellectual function at 4 to 8 years of age. *Neurotoxicology & Teratology, 14, 5,* 1992.

183. Vartiovaara, A., Makela, S., & Pykalainen, R. Effects of parental schizophrenia on children's mental health. *Psychiatria Fennica,* 21, 87-103, 1990.

184. Vereecken, P. *Spatial development.* Groningen, the Netherlands: J.B. Wolters, 1961.

185. Vohr, B.R., Coll, C.G., Lobato, D., Yunis, K.A., & others. Neurodevelopmental and medical status of low-birthweight survivors of bronchopulmonary dysplasia at 10 to 12 years of age. *Developmental Medicine & Child Neurology,* Aug., 1991

186. Webb, J. A follow-up study of cross-cultural validity of the Developmental Test of Visual-Motor Integration. *Perceptual & Motor Skills,* 58, 183-188, 1984.

187. Webb, J., & Abe, K. Cross-cultural validity of the Developmental Test of Visual- Motor Integration. *Perceptual & Motor Skills,* 60, 163-167, 1985.

188. Weerdenburg, G., & Janzen, H.L. Predicting Grade 1 success with a selected kindergarten screening battery. *School Psychology International,* 6, 1, 13-23, 1985.

189. Weil, M.J., & Amundson, S.J. Relationship between visuomotor and handwriting skills of children in kindergarten. *American Journal of Occupational Therapy,* 48, 11, 982-988, 1994.

190. Werner, H. *Comparative psychology of mental development.* NYC: International Universities Press, 1957.

191. Wertheimer, M. Studies in the theory of Gestalt psychology. *Psychol. Forsch.,* 4, 301-350, 1923.

192. Williams, H.G. *Perceptual and motor development.* Englewood Cliffs, NJ: Prentice-Hall, 1983.

193. Williams, J., Zolten A.J., Rickert, V.I., Spence, G.T., & Ashcraft, E.W. Use of nonverbal tests to screen for writing dysfluency in school-age children. *Perceptual and Motor Skills,* 76, 3, (Pt 1), 803-809, 1993.

194. Williams, J., & Ashcraft, E.W. The use of neuropsychological data to detect altered neurological functioning in a child with myelomeningocele. *Journal of Developmental & Behavioral Pediatrics,* 14, 6, 401-404, 1993.

195. Williams, J., & Dykman, R.A. Nonverbal factors derived from children's performances on neuropsychological test instruments. *Developmental Neuropsychology,* 10, 1, 19-26, 1994.

196. Wills, K.E., Holmbeck, G.N., Dillon, K., & McLone, D.G. Intelligence and achievement in children with myelomeningocele. *Journal of Pediatric Psychology,* 15, 2, 161-176, 1990.

197. Winneke, G., Brockhaus, A., Ewers, U., Kramer, U., & others. Results from the European multicenter study on lead neurotoxicity in children: Implications for risk assessment. *Neurotoxicology & Teratology,* 12, 5, 553-559, 1990

198. Wright, B.D., & Stone, M.H. *Best Test Design: Rasch Measurement.* Chicago: Mesa Press, 1979.

199. Wright, G., & DeMers, S.T. Comparison of the relationship between two measures of visual-motor coordination and academic achievement. *Psychology in the Schools,* 19, 473-477, 1982.

200. Ysseldyke, J.E., et al. Similarities and differences between low achievers and students classified learning disabled. *Journal of Special Education,* 16, 73-85, 1982.

201. Zeidner, M., & Most, R. (Eds.) *Psychological testing: An inside view.* Palo Alto: Consulting Psychologists Press, 1992.

202. Zelkowitz, P., Papageorgiou, A., & Allard, M. Relationship of rehospitalization to cognitive and behavioral outcomes in very low birth weight and normal birth weight children. *Journal of Developmental & Behavioral Pediatrics,* 15, 3, 179-185, 1994.

203. Zelkowitz, P., Papageorgiou, A., Zelazo, P.R., & Weiss, M.J. Behavioral adjustment in very low and normal birth weight children. *Journal of Clinical Child Psychology,* 24, 1, 21-30, 1995.

204. Zubek, J.P., & Solberg, P.A. *Human development.* NYC: McGraw-Hill, 1954.

Norms

Norm Alternatives

Age equivalents for *VMI* raw scores are shown in Table 13, page 145. Percentiles and standard scores for raw scores are provided by chronological age levels in Table 14, pages 146-175. Conversions from *VMI* standard scores to NCE's, T-scores, scaled scores, and percentiles are provided in Table 15, page 176.

As with any age or grade equivalents, *VMI* age equivalents should be used judiciously, if at all, for informal communication purposes. Percentiles and standard scores are more reliable and valid measures of individual and group results (1,2,157,158,201). The use of *VMI* standard scores is strongly recommended.

VMI standard scores, like the *Wechsler* scales, have a mean of 100 and a standard deviation of 15 for all age groups and are based upon the means of raw score distributions.

Very Young Children

The *VMI* was designed to focus on early identification of pre-school through primary school children. In addition to the following normative information for very young children, please see the Developmental Comments for the scoring of individual *VMI* shapes, which are shown in Chapter III.

Table 12. Age Norms for Very Young Children

Age	Behavior	Source
28 weeks	Discrimination of vertical-horizontal cross, circle, square, & triangle	Gesell & Ilg (64)
0-8	Watches examiner scribble	Griffiths (70)
1-0	Holds pencil as if to mark	
1-1	Marks in response to demonstration	
1-4	Scribbles freely	
1-9	Imitates* vertical lines	Beery (8)
2-6	Imitates horizontal lines	
2-9	Imitates circular lines	
2-10	Copies* vertical line	
3-0	Copies horizontal line	
3-0	Copies circle	
3-6	Imitates oblique cross	Stanford-Binet (174)

*The word *imitates* is used when a child is asked to copy a form after an examiner has demonstrated how to draw it. The word *copies* is used when a child directly reproduces a geometric form without a demonstration.

Table 13: VMI Raw Score Age Equivalents*

(See page 143 regarding the use of age equivalents.)

Raw	VMI*	Visual*	Motor	Raw
27	-	-	-	27
26	-	>14-2	>15-6	26
25	>14-0	14-2	15-6	25
24	14-0	12-11	12-9	24
23	12-3	11-9	11-2	23
22	11-3	10-6	10-0	22
21	10-3	9-8	9-2	21
20	9-6	8-11	8-6	20
19	8-9	8-3	7-11	19
18	8-1	7-8	7-3	18
17	7-6	7-0	6-9	17
16	7-0	6-6	6-4	16
15	6-6	6-1	6-0	15
14	6-2	5-7	5-7	14
13	5-10	5-1	5-2	13
12	5-6	4-9	4-10	12
11	5-2	4-5	4-6	11
10	4-10	4-0	4-1	10
9	4-6	3-9	3-9	9
8	4-2	3-5	3-5	8
7	3-10	3-0	3-1	7
6	3-6	<3-0	<3-0	6
5	3-1	-	-	5
4	2-11	-	-	4
3	2-9	-	-	3
2	2-6	-	-	2
1	2-0	-	-	1
0	<2-0	-	-	0

* Up to 3 consecutive forms receiving No Score.

VMI Raw	3-0 through 3-1	3-2 through 3-3	3-4 through 3-5	3-6 through 3-7	3-8 through 3-9	3-10 through 3-11
27	·	·	·	·	·	·
26	·	·	·	·	·	·
25	·	·	·	·	·	·
24	·	·	·	·	·	·
23	·	·	·	·	·	·
22	·	·	·	·	·	·
21	·	·	·	·	·	·
20	·	·	·	·	·	·
19	·	·	·	·	·	·
18	·	·	·	·	·	·
17	·	·	·	·	·	·
16	·	·	·	·	·	·
15	·	·	·	·	·	·
14	·	·	·	·	·	155
13	·	·	·	155	155	149
12	·	·	155	154	149	143
11	·	155	153	147	141	135
10	155	151	146	140	134	129
9	145	140	135	130	125	120
8	137	132	127	122	117	112
7	122	118	114	110	106	102
6	112	108	104	100	96	92
5	99	96	93	90	87	84
4	82	80	79	77	75	74
3	76	74	72	70	68	66
2	59	58	57	57	57	56
1	48	47	47	47	47	47
0	·	·	·	·	·	·

VISUAL Raw	3-0 through 3-3	3-4 through 3-7	3-8 through 3-11	MOTOR Raw	3-0 through 3-3	3-4 through 3-7	3-8 through 3-11
27	•	•	•	27	•	•	•
26	•	•	•	26	•	•	•
25	•	•	•	25	•	•	•
24	•	•	•	24	•	•	•
23	•	•	•	23	•	•	•
22	•	•	•	22	•	•	•
21	•	•	•	21	•	•	•
20	•	155	155	20	•	•	•
19	155	153	150	19	•	•	•
18	144	142	140	18	•	•	155
17	139	136	133	17	•	155	149
16	134	131	128	16	155	150	142
15	130	127	124	15	146	140	134
14	125	122	119	14	145	137	129
13	123	119	115	13	137	130	123
12	116	113	110	12	126	121	116
11	114	110	106	11	120	115	110
10	109	105	101	10	115	110	105
9	107	102	97	9	109	104	99
8	103	97	91	8	104	99	94
7	99	93	87	7	100	95	90
6	93	88	83	6	95	90	85
5	90	84	78	5	87	83	79
4	86	79	72	4	81	77	73
3	83	76	69	3	78	73	68
2	80	72	64	2	72	68	64
1	74	67	60	1	66	62	58
0	•	•	•	0	•	•	•

Please see page 176 for conversions to percentiles and other scaled scores.

VMI Raw	4-0 through 4-1	4-2 through 4-3	4-4 through 4-5	4-6 through 4-7	4-8 through 4-9	4-10 through 4-11
27	•	•	•	•	•	•
26	•	•	•	•	•	•
25	•	•	•	•	•	•
24	•	•	•	•	•	•
23	•	•	•	•	•	•
22	•	•	•	•	•	•
21	•	•	•	•	•	•
20	•	•	•	•	•	•
19	•	•	•	•	•	•
18	•	•	•	•	•	155
17	•	•	155	155	155	153
16	•	155	154	150	146	142
15	155	152	145	141	138	135
14	150	144	136	132	129	126
13	144	138	130	126	123	120
12	138	132	125	121	118	114
11	130	124	116	112	109	106
10	123	117	110	106	103	100
9	115	110	104	100	97	93
8	107	102	96	92	89	86
7	99	95	90	87	84	80
6	89	85	80	77	75	72
5	82	79	75	73	70	67
4	72	70	68	67	64	60
3	64	62	59	58	56	54
2	56	55	54	54	45	45
1	47	46	46	46	•	•
0	•	•	•	•	•	•

VISUAL Raw	4-0 through 4-3	4-4 through 4-7	4-8 through 4-11		MOTOR Raw	4-0 through 4-3	4-4 through 4-7	4-8 through 4-11
27	•	•	•		27	•	•	•
26	•	•	•		26	•	•	•
25	•	•	•		25	•	•	•
24	•	•	•		24	•	•	•
23	•	•	•		23	•	•	•
22	•	•	•		22	•	155	155
21	•	155	155		21	•	148	146
20	155	153	148		20	155	144	140
19	146	143	140		19	153	140	135
18	137	135	132		18	147	136	131
17	130	127	125		17	138	128	124
16	126	123	120		16	133	125	121
15	121	118	114		15	127	121	116
14	115	112	109		14	121	113	109
13	110	106	102		13	116	110	105
12	106	103	98		12	110	105	101
11	101	97	92		11	105	100	96
10	96	92	87		10	100	95	90
9	92	87	81		9	95	90	85
8	85	80	74		8	90	85	80
7	81	75	69		7	84	79	74
6	77	72	65		6	80	75	70
5	71	65	58		5	75	71	66
4	65	58	53		4	69	65	60
3	62	56	45		3	64	59	55
2	56	48	•		2	60	56	52
1	52	45	•		1	54	50	48
0	•	•	•		0	•	•	•

VMI Raw	5-0 through 5-1	5-2 through 5-3	5-4 through 5-5	5-6 through 5-7	5-8 through 5-9	5-10 through 5-11
27	·	·	·	·	·	·
26	·	·	·	·	·	·
25	·	·	·	·	·	·
24	·	·	·	·	·	·
23	·	·	·	·	·	·
22	·	·	·	·	·	·
21	·	·	·	·	·	·
20	·	·	·	·	·	·
19	·	·	·	·	155	155
18	155	155	155	155	151	145
17	151	148	144	142	137	132
16	139	135	130	127	124	120
15	132	128	124	122	118	115
14	123	119	115	113	110	106
13	117	114	110	108	105	101
12	111	108	103	101	98	94
11	103	99	95	93	90	86
10	97	93	89	87	84	80
9	90	86	81	79	76	72
8	83	80	76	74	71	68
7	77	73	68	66	63	60
6	70	67	64	62	59	56
5	64	60	56	54	52	50
4	57	54	49	47	46	45
3	52	49	47	45	45	·
2	49	47	45	·	·	·
1	45	45	·	·	·	·
0	·	·	·	·	·	·

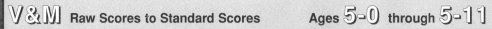

VISUAL Raw	5-0 through 5-3	5-4 through 5-7	5-8 through 5-11	MOTOR Raw	5-0 through 5-3	5-4 through 5-7	5-8 through 5-11
27	•	•	•	27	•	•	•
26	•	•	•	26	•	•	•
25	•	•	•	25	•	•	•
24	•	•	•	24	•	•	155
23	•	155	155	23	155	155	150
22	155	154	150	22	154	152	142
21	151	146	142	21	144	142	135
20	143	138	134	20	136	132	126
19	136	133	129	19	131	126	121
18	129	126	121	18	127	122	117
17	123	121	116	17	121	117	112
16	116	113	109	16	116	112	107
15	111	107	102	15	112	107	102
14	105	102	97	14	106	102	98
13	98	94	90	13	101	96	93
12	93	88	83	12	96	92	89
11	87	82	77	11	91	87	84
10	81	76	71	10	86	81	78
9	75	70	65	9	80	75	73
8	68	62	57	8	76	71	68
7	63	57	53	7	70	65	63
6	57	50	48	6	64	59	58
5	51	45	45	5	61	56	54
4	48	•	•	4	54	49	48
3	45	•	•	3	51	47	46
2	•	•	•	2	49	45	45
1	•	•	•	1	45	•	•
0	•	•	•	0	•	•	•

Please see page 176 for conversions to percentiles and other scaled scores.

VMI Raw	6-0 through 6-1	6-2 through 6-3	6-4 through 6-5	6-6 through 6-7	6-8 through 6-9	6-10 through 6-11
27	•	•	•	•	•	•
26	•	•	•	•	•	•
25	•	•	•	•	•	•
24	•	•	•	•	•	•
23	•	•	•	155	155	155
22	•	•	155	154	152	150
21	•	155	155	145	142	139
20	155	153	145	136	133	130
19	150	142	135	127	125	122
18	139	132	126	120	118	115
17	128	123	118	113	111	109
16	117	113	110	106	104	101
15	111	107	104	100	98	96
14	103	100	96	93	91	89
13	98	94	91	87	85	83
12	91	87	84	80	78	76
11	83	80	76	73	71	69
10	77	73	70	66	64	63
9	69	65	62	58	56	55
8	65	61	58	55	53	52
7	57	53	50	47	46	46
6	54	51	48	45	45	45
5	49	47	45	•	•	•
4	45	45	•	•	•	•
3	•	•	•	•	•	•
2	•	•	•	•	•	•
1	•	•	•	•	•	•
0	•	•	•	•	•	•

Please see page 176 for conversions to percentiles and other scaled scores.

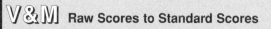

VISUAL Raw	6-0 through 6-3	6-4 through 6-7	6-8 through 6-11	MOTOR Raw	6-0 through 6-3	6-4 through 6-7	6-8 through 6-11
27	•	•	•	27	•	•	•
26	•	155	155	26	•	155	155
25	•	153	152	25	155	145	144
24	155	149	147	24	145	132	131
23	150	145	141	23	138	127	126
22	145	141	137	22	132	123	121
21	137	133	129	21	127	120	117
20	130	126	122	20	120	114	112
19	125	121	117	19	115	110	108
18	117	112	109	18	112	107	104
17	112	107	103	17	108	103	100
16	104	100	96	16	103	98	96
15	97	92	89	15	98	93	91
14	91	86	83	14	94	90	88
13	86	82	78	13	90	87	84
12	79	74	70	12	85	82	80
11	72	67	64	11	80	77	75
10	65	60	57	10	76	73	71
9	61	56	52	9	70	68	66
8	53	48	46	8	66	63	61
7	49	45	45	7	60	58	57
6	45	•	•	6	57	56	54
5	•	•	•	5	53	51	50
4	•	•	•	4	48	47	46
3	•	•	•	3	46	45	45
2	•	•	•	2	45	•	•
1	•	•	•	1	•	•	•
0	•	•	•	0	•	•	•

Please see page 176 for conversions to percentiles and other scaled scores.

VMI Raw	7-0 through 7-1	7-2 through 7-3	7-4 through 7-5	7-6 through 7-7	7-8 through 7-9	7-10 through 7-11
27	•	•	•	•	•	•
26	•	•	•	•	•	•
25	•	•	•	•	•	•
24	•	•	•	•	155	155
23	155	155	155	155	152	148
22	148	145	143	141	138	135
21	136	132	129	126	125	123
20	128	125	122	119	118	116
19	120	118	115	113	111	110
18	113	111	108	106	104	103
17	107	104	102	100	98	97
16	99	97	94	92	91	89
15	94	91	89	87	85	84
14	87	85	83	81	80	78
13	81	78	76	74	73	71
12	74	72	70	68	66	64
11	67	65	63	61	60	58
10	61	59	58	56	55	53
9	53	51	50	48	48	47
8	50	48	47	45	45	45
7	45	45	45	•	•	•
6	•	•	•	•	•	•
5	•	•	•	•	•	•
4	•	•	•	•	•	•
3	•	•	•	•	•	•
2	•	•	•	•	•	•
1	•	•	•	•	•	•
0	•	•	•	•	•	•

    Please see page 176 for conversions to percentiles and other scaled scores.

VISUAL Raw	7-0 through 7-3	7-4 through 7-7	7-8 through 7-11
27	155	155	155
26	152	150	147
25	150	149	144
24	144	142	137
23	138	134	130
22	132	128	124
21	126	122	117
20	117	113	110
19	112	108	104
18	105	102	98
17	98	94	90
16	92	88	84
15	85	82	78
14	79	76	72
13	75	71	66
12	66	62	58
11	60	57	53
10	53	50	48
9	49	45	45
8	45	•	•
7	•	•	•
6	•	•	•
5	•	•	•
4	•	•	•
3	•	•	•
2	•	•	•
1	•	•	•
0	•	•	•

MOTOR Raw	7-0 through 7-3	7-4 through 7-7	7-8 through 7-11
27	•	•	155
26	155	155	151
25	143	142	137
24	129	128	125
23	124	123	120
22	120	118	115
21	115	112	109
20	109	107	105
19	105	103	101
18	101	98	96
17	98	95	93
16	93	91	90
15	89	87	86
14	85	83	82
13	81	78	77
12	77	75	74
11	74	72	71
10	69	67	66
9	64	62	61
8	60	58	57
7	57	56	55
6	53	51	50
5	49	48	47
4	46	45	45
3	45	•	•
2	•	•	•
1	•	•	•
0	•	•	•

Please see page 176 for conversions to percentiles and other scaled scores.

VMI Raw	8-0 through 8-1	8-2 through 8-3	8-4 through 8-5	8-6 through 8-7	8-8 through 8-9	8-10 through 8-11
27	•	•	•	•	•	•
26	•	•	•	•	•	155
25	•	155	155	155	155	152
24	155	154	149	145	143	140
23	145	141	137	133	131	129
22	132	129	126	123	121	120
21	122	120	119	117	115	114
20	115	113	112	110	108	107
19	108	106	105	103	101	100
18	101	99	98	96	94	93
17	95	93	92	90	89	87
16	88	86	85	83	82	80
15	82	80	79	77	76	75
14	77	75	74	72	71	69
13	70	68	67	65	64	63
12	63	61	59	57	56	55
11	57	56	54	53	52	50
10	52	50	49	47	46	46
9	47	46	46	45	45	45
8	45	45	45	•	•	•
7	•	•	•	•	•	•
6	•	•	•	•	•	•
5	•	•	•	•	•	•
4	•	•	•	•	•	•
3	•	•	•	•	•	•
2	•	•	•	•	•	•
1	•	•	•	•	•	•
0	•	•	•	•	•	•

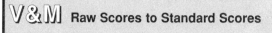

VISUAL Raw	8-0 through 8-3	8-4 through 8-7	8-8 through 8-11
27	154	152	147
26	145	142	138
25	140	135	132
24	133	128	125
23	127	123	120
22	119	115	112
21	113	108	106
20	106	103	100
19	99	95	93
18	94	90	87
17	87	83	81
16	80	76	74
15	75	71	68
14	67	63	61
13	62	57	56
12	54	50	49
11	49	45	45
10	45	•	•
9	•	•	•
8	•	•	•
7	•	•	•
6	•	•	•
5	•	•	•
4	•	•	•
3	•	•	•
2	•	•	•
1	•	•	•
0	•	•	•

MOTOR Raw	8-0 through 8-3	8-4 through 8-7	8-8 through 8-11
27	155	155	149
26	147	142	135
25	131	126	122
24	121	118	116
23	116	113	111
22	113	110	107
21	107	104	102
20	102	100	99
19	98	96	95
18	95	93	91
17	92	90	88
16	88	87	85
15	84	83	81
14	81	80	78
13	76	75	74
12	73	72	70
11	69	68	66
10	66	65	63
9	61	60	59
8	57	56	55
7	55	54	52
6	49	48	48
5	46	45	45
4	45	•	•
3	•	•	•
2	•	•	•
1	•	•	•
0	•	•	•

Please see page 176 for conversions to percentiles and other scaled scores.

VMI Raw	9-0 through 9-1	9-2 through 9-3	9-4 through 9-5	9-6 through 9-7	9-8 through 9-9	9-10 through 9-11
27	•	•	•	•	155	155
26	155	155	155	155	154	152
25	150	148	145	143	141	138
24	138	135	133	130	128	127
23	127	124	122	120	119	117
22	118	116	115	113	112	110
21	112	110	109	107	105	104
20	105	103	102	100	98	97
19	98	96	95	93	91	89
18	91	89	88	86	84	83
17	86	85	83	82	80	78
16	79	78	76	75	73	71
15	74	72	71	70	68	65
14	68	66	65	63	61	58
13	62	60	59	58	56	54
12	54	52	51	50	49	48
11	49	48	46	45	45	45
10	45	45	45	•	•	•
9	•	•	•	•	•	•
8	•	•	•	•	•	•
7	•	•	•	•	•	•
6	•	•	•	•	•	•
5	•	•	•	•	•	•
4	•	•	•	•	•	•
3	•	•	•	•	•	•
2	•	•	•	•	•	•
1	•	•	•	•	•	•
0	•	•	•	•	•	•

Please see page 176 for conversions to percentiles and other scaled scores.

VISUAL Raw	9-0 through 9-3	9-4 through 9-7	9-8 through 9-11
27	143	138	135
26	134	130	128
25	129	126	124
24	123	120	117
23	116	113	111
22	109	106	104
21	103	101	99
20	96	93	91
19	90	88	86
18	85	82	79
17	78	76	74
16	73	71	69
15	66	63	61
14	60	58	57
13	55	54	52
12	47	46	46
11	45	45	45
10	•	•	•
9	•	•	•
8	•	•	•
7	•	•	•
6	•	•	•
5	•	•	•
4	•	•	•
3	•	•	•
2	•	•	•
1	•	•	•
0	•	•	•

MOTOR Raw	9-0 through 9-3	9-4 through 9-7	9-8 through 9-11
27	139	130	128
26	127	120	118
25	117	113	112
24	113	111	110
23	108	106	105
22	105	102	101
21	100	98	97
20	97	96	95
19	93	92	91
18	89	87	86
17	87	85	84
16	82	80	79
15	79	77	76
14	76	74	73
13	72	71	70
12	69	67	66
11	65	63	61
10	61	59	58
9	58	57	55
8	55	54	52
7	51	49	48
6	47	47	46
5	45	45	45
4	•	•	•
3	•	•	•
2	•	•	•
1	•	•	•
0	•	•	•

Please see page 176 for conversions to percentiles and other scaled scores.

VMI Raw Scores to Standard Scores — Ages 10-0 through 10-11

VMI Raw	10-0 through 10-1	10-2 through 10-3	10-4 through 10-5	10-6 through 10-7	10-8 through 10-9	10-10 through 10-11
27	155	155	155	155	155	155
26	151	149	147	145	143	141
25	136	134	131	129	128	127
24	125	123	122	120	119	117
23	116	115	113	112	111	110
22	109	108	106	105	104	102
21	102	100	99	97	96	94
20	95	93	92	90	89	88
19	88	86	84	82	81	80
18	81	79	78	76	75	75
17	76	74	72	70	69	68
16	69	66	64	62	61	60
15	63	60	58	55	55	54
14	56	53	51	48	48	47
13	52	49	47	45	45	45
12	47	45	45	•	•	•
11	45	•	•	•	•	•
10	•	•	•	•	•	•
9	•	•	•	•	•	•
8	•	•	•	•	•	•
7	•	•	•	•	•	•
6	•	•	•	•	•	•
5	•	•	•	•	•	•
4	•	•	•	•	•	•
3	•	•	•	•	•	•
2	•	•	•	•	•	•
1	•	•	•	•	•	•
0	•	•	•	•	•	•

Please see page 176 for conversions to percentiles and other scaled scores.

VISUAL Raw	10-0 through 10-3	10-4 through 10-7	10-8 through 10-11	MOTOR Raw	10-0 through 10-3	10-4 through 10-7	10-8 through 10-11
27	131	128	127	27	125	123	121
26	126	124	123	26	115	113	112
25	121	119	117	25	111	110	109
24	115	112	110	24	108	107	106
23	108	106	105	23	104	103	101
22	102	100	98	22	99	98	97
21	97	95	93	21	97	96	95
20	90	88	87	20	93	92	91
19	85	83	81	19	89	88	87
18	75	72	72	18	86	85	84
17	73	71	70	17	82	81	80
16	67	65	64	16	77	76	76
15	60	58	58	15	75	74	73
14	56	55	53	14	72	71	70
13	50	48	47	13	68	67	65
12	45	45	45	12	64	63	62
11	•	•	•	11	60	58	58
10	•	•	•	10	57	56	55
9	•	•	•	9	54	52	51
8	•	•	•	8	50	48	47
7	•	•	•	7	47	46	46
6	•	•	•	6	46	45	45
5	•	•	•	5	45	•	•
4	•	•	•	4	•	•	•
3	•	•	•	3	•	•	•
2	•	•	•	2	•	•	•
1	•	•	•	1	•	•	•
0	•	•	•	0	•	•	•

Please see page 176 for conversions to percentiles and other scaled scores.

VMI Raw	11-0 through 11-1	11-2 through 11-3	11-4 through 11-5	11-6 through 11-7	11-8 through 11-9	11-10 through 11-11
27	154	151	149	146	146	145
26	140	138	136	134	133	132
25	126	124	123	122	121	120
24	116	115	113	112	111	110
23	109	107	106	105	104	103
22	101	100	98	97	96	95
21	93	92	90	89	88	88
20	87	85	84	83	83	82
19	80	79	78	77	77	76
18	74	73	73	72	71	71
17	67	66	65	64	63	63
16	60	59	58	57	56	56
15	54	53	53	52	51	51
14	47	46	46	45	45	45
13	45	45	45	•	•	•
12	•	•	•	•	•	•
11	•	•	•	•	•	•
10	•	•	•	•	•	•
9	•	•	•	•	•	•
8	•	•	•	•	•	•
7	•	•	•	•	•	•
6	•	•	•	•	•	•
5	•	•	•	•	•	•
4	•	•	•	•	•	•
3	•	•	•	•	•	•
2	•	•	•	•	•	•
1	•	•	•	•	•	•
0	•	•	•	•	•	•

VISUAL Raw	11-0 through 11-3	11-4 through 11-7	11-8 through 11-11		MOTOR Raw	11-0 through 11-3	11-4 through 11-7	11-8 through 11-11
27	126	125	123		27	120	118	117
26	121	120	118		26	111	110	109
25	114	112	111		25	107	106	106
24	109	107	106		24	104	103	102
23	103	102	100		23	100	98	98
22	97	95	94		22	97	96	95
21	92	90	89		21	93	92	91
20	86	85	83		20	89	88	88
19	80	78	77		19	86	85	85
18	73	73	72		18	83	82	81
17	69	68	66		17	78	77	77
16	62	61	60		16	75	75	74
15	57	57	56		15	72	71	70
14	52	50	49		14	68	67	66
13	47	46	46		13	64	62	62
12	45	45	45		12	60	59	59
11	•	•	•		11	57	57	56
10	•	•	•		10	54	53	52
9	•	•	•		9	49	48	48
8	•	•	•		8	47	46	46
7	•	•	•		7	45	45	45
6	•	•	•		6	•	•	•
5	•	•	•		5	•	•	•
4	•	•	•		4	•	•	•
3	•	•	•		3	•	•	•
2	•	•	•		2	•	•	•
1	•	•	•		1	•	•	•
0	•	•	•		0	•	•	•

Please see page 176 for conversions to percentiles and other scaled scores.

VMI Raw	12-0 through 12-1	12-2 through 12-3	12-4 through 12-5	12-6 through 12-7	12-8 through 12-9	12-10 through 12-11
27	145	144	144	143	142	140
26	131	129	128	127	126	125
25	120	119	118	117	116	115
24	110	109	108	107	106	106
23	102	100	99	98	97	97
22	95	94	93	92	91	90
21	87	86	86	85	85	84
20	82	82	81	81	80	80
19	76	75	75	74	74	73
18	70	69	69	68	67	67
17	62	61	61	60	60	59
16	55	54	54	53	53	53
15	50	49	49	48	48	47
14	45	45	45	45	45	45
13	•	•	•	•	•	•
12	•	•	•	•	•	•
11	•	•	•	•	•	•
10	•	•	•	•	•	•
9	•	•	•	•	•	•
8	•	•	•	•	•	•
7	•	•	•	•	•	•
6	•	•	•	•	•	•
5	•	•	•	•	•	•
4	•	•	•	•	•	•
3	•	•	•	•	•	•
2	•	•	•	•	•	•
1	•	•	•	•	•	•
0	•	•	•	•	•	•

Please see page 176 for conversions to percentiles and other scaled scores

VISUAL Raw	12-0 through 12-3	12-4 through 12-7	12-8 through 12-11	MOTOR Raw	12-0 through 12-3	12-4 through 12-7	12-8 through 12-11
27	122	120	118	27	116	115	114
26	115	113	112	26	109	108	108
25	111	110	108	25	105	105	104
24	104	103	101	24	102	101	100
23	98	96	95	23	97	97	97
22	93	92	90	22	95	94	94
21	88	87	85	21	91	90	90
20	82	80	78	20	87	87	86
19	76	75	74	19	84	84	83
18	71	70	68	18	81	80	79
17	65	63	61	17	76	76	76
16	59	58	57	16	74	73	73
15	56	55	53	15	70	69	69
14	48	47	46	14	66	65	64
13	45	45	45	13	61	61	60
12	•	•	•	12	58	58	58
11	•	•	•	11	56	55	55
10	•	•	•	10	52	51	50
9	•	•	•	9	47	47	47
8	•	•	•	8	46	46	45
7	•	•	•	7	45	45	•
6	•	•	•	6	•	•	•
5	•	•	•	5	•	•	•
4	•	•	•	4	•	•	•
3	•	•	•	3	•	•	•
2	•	•	•	2	•	•	•
1	•	•	•	1	•	•	•
0	•	•	•	0	•	•	•

Please see page 176 for conversions to percentiles and other scaled scores.

VMI Raw	13-0 through 13-1	13-2 through 13-3	13-4 through 13-5	13-6 through 13-7	13-8 through 13-9	13-10 through 13-11
27	139	137	136	134	133	132
26	125	124	123	122	121	120
25	114	112	111	110	110	109
24	105	104	104	103	103	102
23	96	95	95	94	94	94
22	90	89	88	87	87	86
21	84	83	83	82	82	81
20	79	78	78	77	77	76
19	73	72	72	71	71	71
18	66	65	65	64	64	63
17	59	59	58	58	58	58
16	53	52	52	52	52	51
15	47	47	46	46	46	46
14	45	45	45	45	45	45
13	•	•	•	•	•	•
12	•	•	•	•	•	•
11	•	•	•	•	•	•
10	•	•	•	•	•	•
9	•	•	•	•	•	•
8	•	•	•	•	•	•
7	•	•	•	•	•	•
6	•	•	•	•	•	•
5	•	•	•	•	•	•
4	•	•	•	•	•	•
3	•	•	•	•	•	•
2	•	•	•	•	•	•
1	•	•	•	•	•	•
0	•	•	•	•	•	•

Please see page 176 for conversions to percentiles and other scaled scores

SUAL Raw	13-0 through 13-3	13-4 through 13-7	13-8 through 13-11	MOTOR Raw	13-0 through 13-3	13-4 through 13-7	13-8 through 13-11
27	115	113	112	27	113	112	112
26	111	110	108	26	107	107	106
25	106	104	102	25	104	103	103
24	99	97	96	24	100	99	99
23	93	92	90	23	96	96	96
22	89	87	85	22	93	93	92
21	82	80	79	21	89	89	89
20	77	75	74	20	86	86	85
19	72	71	69	19	83	82	82
18	67	65	63	18	79	78	78
17	60	58	57	17	75	75	75
16	55	54	52	16	72	72	71
15	50	48	47	15	68	68	67
14	46	45	45	14	64	63	63
13	45	•	•	13	60	60	59
12	•	•	•	12	57	57	57
11	•	•	•	11	54	54	53
10	•	•	•	10	50	49	49
9	•	•	•	9	47	47	46
8	•	•	•	8	45	45	45
7	•	•	•	7	•	•	•
6	•	•	•	6	•	•	•
5	•	•	•	5	•	•	•
4	•	•	•	4	•	•	•
3	•	•	•	3	•	•	•
2	•	•	•	2	•	•	•
1	•	•	•	1	•	•	•
0	•	•	•	0	•	•	•

ease see page 176 for conversions to percentiles and other scaled scores.

VMI Raw	14-0 through 14-1	14-2 through 14-3	14-4 through 14-5	14-6 through 14-7	14-8 through 14-9	14-10 through 14-11
27	131	129	128	127	127	126
26	120	119	118	117	117	116
25	109	109	108	108	108	108
24	102	101	101	100	100	99
23	94	93	93	93	93	92
22	86	86	85	85	85	84
21	81	81	80	80	80	80
20	76	76	75	75	75	75
19	71	70	70	70	70	69
18	63	62	62	61	61	61
17	58	57	57	57	57	57
16	51	50	50	49	49	49
15	46	45	45	45	45	45
14	45	•	•	•	•	•
13	•	•	•	•	•	•
12	•	•	•	•	•	•
11	•	•	•	•	•	•
10	•	•	•	•	•	•
9	•	•	•	•	•	•
8	•	•	•	•	•	•
7	•	•	•	•	•	•
6	•	•	•	•	•	•
5	•	•	•	•	•	•
4	•	•	•	•	•	•
3	•	•	•	•	•	•
2	•	•	•	•	•	•
1	•	•	•	•	•	•
0	•	•	•	•	•	•

Please see page 176 for conversions to percentiles and other scaled scores

VISUAL Raw	14-0 through 14-3	14-4 through 14-7	14-8 through 14-11	MOTOR Raw	14-0 through 14-3	14-4 through 14-7	14-8 through 14-11
27	111	110	109	27	111	110	110
26	105	103	103	26	106	105	105
25	100	98	97	25	102	102	101
24	94	93	92	24	99	98	98
23	89	87	86	23	95	95	94
22	83	81	81	22	92	91	91
21	77	76	75	21	88	88	87
20	73	72	71	20	85	84	84
19	67	65	64	19	81	81	80
18	61	59	58	18	78	77	77
17	57	56	55	17	74	74	73
16	50	48	47	16	71	70	70
15	46	45	45	15	66	66	65
14	45	•	•	14	62	62	61
13	•	•	•	13	59	59	58
12	•	•	•	12	56	56	55
11	•	•	•	11	53	52	51
10	•	•	•	10	49	48	48
9	•	•	•	9	46	45	45
8	•	•	•	8	45	•	•
7	•	•	•	7	•	•	•
6	•	•	•	6	•	•	•
5	•	•	•	5	•	•	•
4	•	•	•	4	•	•	•
3	•	•	•	3	•	•	•
2	•	•	•	2	•	•	•
1	•	•	•	1	•	•	•
0	•	•	•	0	•	•	•

Please see page 176 for conversions to percentiles and other scaled scores.

VMI Raw	15-0 through 15-1	15-2 through 15-3	15-4 through 15-5	15-6 through 15-7	15-8 through 15-9	15-10 through 15-11
27	126	126	125	125	125	124
26	116	115	115	114	114	114
25	108	107	107	107	107	106
24	99	98	98	97	97	97
23	92	91	91	90	90	89
22	84	84	83	83	83	83
21	80	79	79	79	78	78
20	75	74	74	74	74	73
19	69	69	68	68	68	67
18	61	60	60	60	60	59
17	57	56	56	56	56	55
16	49	48	48	48	48	47
15	45	45	45	45	45	45
14	•	•	•	•	•	•
13	•	•	•	•	•	•
12	•	•	•	•	•	•
11	•	•	•	•	•	•
10	•	•	•	•	•	•
9	•	•	•	•	•	•
8	•	•	•	•	•	•
7	•	•	•	•	•	•
6	•	•	•	•	•	•
5	•	•	•	•	•	•
4	•	•	•	•	•	•
3	•	•	•	•	•	•
2	•	•	•	•	•	•
1	•	•	•	•	•	•
0	•	•	•	•	•	•

Please see page 176 for conversions to percentiles and other scaled score

VISUAL Raw	15-0 through 15-3	15-4 through 15-7	15-8 through 15-11
27	107	107	106
26	102	102	101
25	96	96	95
24	90	90	89
23	84	84	83
22	80	80	79
21	74	74	73
20	68	68	67
19	61	61	60
18	56	56	56
17	52	52	51
16	46	46	45
15	45	45	•
14	•	•	•
13	•	•	•
12	•	•	•
11	•	•	•
10	•	•	•
9	•	•	•
8	•	•	•
7	•	•	•
6	•	•	•
5	•	•	•
4	•	•	•
3	•	•	•
2	•	•	•
1	•	•	•
0	•	•	•

MOTOR Raw	15-0 through 15-3	15-4 through 15-7	15-8 through 15-11
27	109	108	108
26	104	104	104
25	101	100	100
24	97	97	96
23	94	93	93
22	90	90	89
21	87	86	86
20	83	83	82
19	80	79	79
18	76	76	75
17	73	72	72
16	69	68	68
15	65	64	64
14	61	61	60
13	58	57	57
12	55	54	54
11	51	51	50
10	47	46	46
9	45	45	45
8	45	•	•
7	•	•	•
6	•	•	•
5	•	•	•
4	•	•	•
3	•	•	•
2	•	•	•
1	•	•	•
0	•	•	•

Please see page 176 for conversions to percentiles and other scaled scores.

VMI Raw	16-0 through 16-1	16-2 through 16-3	16-4 through 16-5	16-6 through 16-7	16-8 through 16-9	16-10 through 16-11
27	124	124	123	123	123	122
26	114	113	113	113	113	112
25	106	106	105	105	105	104
24	97	96	96	96	96	95
23	89	88	88	87	87	86
22	83	82	82	82	82	81
21	77	76	76	75	75	74
20	73	73	72	72	72	71
19	67	67	66	66	66	65
18	59	59	58	58	58	57
17	55	55	54	54	54	53
16	47	47	46	46	46	45
15	45	45	45	45	45	•
14	•	•	•	•	•	•
13	•	•	•	•	•	•
12	•	•	•	•	•	•
11	•	•	•	•	•	•
10	•	•	•	•	•	•
9	•	•	•	•	•	•
8	•	•	•	•	•	•
7	•	•	•	•	•	•
6	•	•	•	•	•	•
5	•	•	•	•	•	•
4	•	•	•	•	•	•
3	•	•	•	•	•	•
2	•	•	•	•	•	•
1	•	•	•	•	•	•
0	•	•	•	•	•	•

Please see page 176 for conversions to percentiles and other scaled scores.

VISUAL Raw	16-0 through 16-3	16-4 through 16-7	16-8 through 16-11	MOTOR Raw	16-0 through 16-3	16-4 through 16-7	16-8 through 16-11
27	105	104	103	27	107	107	106
26	101	100	99	26	103	103	102
25	94	93	92	25	99	99	98
24	88	87	86	24	96	95	95
23	83	82	81	23	92	92	91
22	77	76	75	22	89	88	88
21	72	71	71	21	85	85	84
20	67	66	65	20	82	81	81
19	60	59	57	19	78	78	77
18	56	56	53	18	75	74	74
17	49	48	47	17	71	71	70
16	45	45	45	16	67	67	66
15	•	•	•	15	63	63	62
14	•	•	•	14	60	59	59
13	•	•	•	13	57	56	56
12	•	•	•	12	53	53	52
11	•	•	•	11	49	49	48
10	•	•	•	10	45	45	45
9	•	•	•	9	•	•	•
8	•	•	•	8	•	•	•
7	•	•	•	7	•	•	•
6	•	•	•	6	•	•	•
5	•	•	•	5	•	•	•
4	•	•	•	4	•	•	•
3	•	•	•	3	•	•	•
2	•	•	•	2	•	•	•
1	•	•	•	1	•	•	•
0	•	•	•	0	•	•	•

Please see page 176 for conversions to percentiles and other scaled scores.

VMI Raw	17-0 through 17-1	17-2 through 17-3	17-4 through 17-5	17-6 through 17-7	17-8 through 17-9	17-10 through 17-11
27	122	121	121	120	120	119
26	112	112	111	111	111	110
25	104	104	103	103	103	102
24	95	95	94	94	94	93
23	86	86	85	85	85	84
22	81	81	80	80	80	79
21	74	74	73	73	73	72
20	71	71	70	70	70	69
19	65	65	64	64	64	63
18	57	57	56	56	56	55
17	53	53	52	52	52	51
16	45	45	45	45	45	45
15	•	•	•	•	•	•
14	•	•	•	•	•	•
13	•	•	•	•	•	•
12	•	•	•	•	•	•
11	•	•	•	•	•	•
10	•	•	•	•	•	•
9	•	•	•	•	•	•
8	•	•	•	•	•	•
7	•	•	•	•	•	•
6	•	•	•	•	•	•
5	•	•	•	•	•	•
4	•	•	•	•	•	•
3	•	•	•	•	•	•
2	•	•	•	•	•	•
1	•	•	•	•	•	•
0	•	•	•	•	•	•

VISUAL Raw	17-0 through 17-3	17-4 through 17-7	17-8 through 17-11	MOTOR Raw	17-0 through 17-3	17-4 through 17-7	17-8 through 17-11
27	103	102	101	27	105	105	104
26	99	98	97	26	102	101	100
25	92	91	90	25	98	98	97
24	86	85	84	24	94	94	93
23	81	80	79	23	91	91	90
22	75	74	74	22	87	87	86
21	70	70	69	21	84	84	83
20	64	63	62	20	80	80	79
19	56	54	53	19	77	76	76
18	50	47	46	18	73	73	72
17	46	45	45	17	70	69	69
16	45	•	•	16	66	65	65
15	•	•	•	15	62	61	61
14	•	•	•	14	59	58	57
13	•	•	•	13	55	55	54
12	•	•	•	12	52	51	50
11	•	•	•	11	47	46	46
10	•	•	•	10	45	45	45
9	•	•	•	9	•	•	•
8	•	•	•	8	•	•	•
7	•	•	•	7	•	•	•
6	•	•	•	6	•	•	•
5	•	•	•	5	•	•	•
4	•	•	•	4	•	•	•
3	•	•	•	3	•	•	•
2	•	•	•	2	•	•	•
1	•	•	•	1	•	•	•
0	•	•	•	0	•	•	•

Please see page 176 for conversions to percentiles and other scaled scores.

Table 15. Standard Score conversions to Percentiles and other Scaled Scores.

SS	NCE's	T-Scores	Scaled Scores	%ile Ranks	SS	NCE's	T-Scores	Scaled Scores	%ile Ranks
X=100 SD=15	X=50 SD=21.06	X=50 SD=10	X=10 SD=3		X=100 SD=15	X=50 SD=21.06	X=50 SD=10	X=10 SD=3	
155	99+	80+	20+	99.98					
154	99+	80+	20	99.97	99	49	49	10	47
153	99+	80+	20	99.96	98	47	49	10	45
152	99+	80+	20	99.95	97	46	48	9	42
151	99+	80+	20	99.94	96	44	47	9	39
150	99+	80+	20	99.93	95	43	47	9	37
149	99+	80+	19	99.92	94	42	46	9	34
148	99+	80+	19	99.91	93	40	45	9	32
147	99+	80+	19	99.9	92	39	45	8	30
146	99+	80+	19	99.8	91	37	44	8	27
145	99+	80	19	99.7	90	36	43	8	25
144	99+	79	19	99.6	89	35	43	8	23
143	99+	79	19	99.5	88	33	42	8	21
142	99+	78	18	99.4	87	32	41	7	19
141	99+	77	18	99.3	86	30	41	7	18
140	99+	77	18	99.2	85	29	40	7	16
139	99+	76	18	99.1	84	28	39	7	14
138	99	75	18	99	83	26	39	7	13
137	99	75	17	99	82	25	38	6	12
136	99	74	17	99	81	23	37	6	10
135	99	73	17	99	80	22	37	6	9
134	98	73	17	99	79	21	36	6	8
133	96	72	17	99	78	19	35	6	7
132	95	71	16	98	77	18	35	5	6
131	94	71	16	98	76	16	34	5	5
130	92	70	16	98	75	15	33	5	5
129	91	69	16	97	74	13	33	5	4
128	89	69	16	97	73	12	32	5	4
127	88	68	15	96	72	11	31	4	3
126	87	67	15	96	71	9	31	4	3
125	85	67	15	95	70	8	30	4	2
124	84	66	15	95	69	6	29	4	2
123	82	65	15	94	68	5	*29	4	2
122	81	65	14	93	67	4	28	3	1
121	79	64	14	92	66	2	27	3	1
120	78	63	14	91	65	1	27	3	1
119	77	63	14	90	64	1	26	3	1
118	75	62	14	88	63	1	25	3	1
117	74	61	13	87	62	1	25	2	1
116	72	61	13	86	61	1-	24	2	.9
115	71	60	13	84	60	1-	23	2	.8
114	70	59	13	82	59	1-	23	2	.7
113	68	59	13	81	58	1-	22	2	.6
112	67	58	12	79	57	1-	21	1	.5
111	65	57	12	77	56	1-	21	1	.4
110	64	57	12	75	55	1-	20	1	.3
109	63	56	12	73	54	1-	20	1	.2
108	61	55	12	70	53	1-	20	1	.1
107	60	55	11	68	52	1-	20-	1-	.09
106	58	53	11	65	51	1-	20-	1-	.08
105	57	53	11	63	50	1-	20-	1-	.07
104	56	53	11	61	49	1-	20-	1-	.06
103	54	52	11	58	48	1-	20-	1-	.05
102	53	51	10	55	47	1-	20-	1-	.04
101	51	51	10	53	46	1-	20-	1-	.03
100	50	50	10	50	45	1-	20-	1-	.02